SCHOOL of SEWING

Learn it. Teach it.
Sew Together.

SEWING

SHEA HENDERSON

Published in 2014 by Lucky Spool Media, LLC

Lucky Spool Media, LLC
1005 Blackwood Lane, Lafayette CA 94549
www.luckyspool.com
info@luckyspool.com

TEXT © Shea Henderson
EDITOR Susanne Woods
ILLUSTRATIONS Kari Vojtechovsky
PHOTOGRAPHY Lauren Hunt
STYLING Lauren Hunt
DESIGNER Rae Ann Spitzenberger

Photograph on page 83 of Jeni Baker
© Michael Hanna
Photograph on page 95 of Alex Ledgerwood
© Lauren Hunt

9 8 7 6 5 4 3 2 1

First Edition
Printed and bound in the USA

Library of Congress Cataloging-in-Publication
Data available upon request

LSID 0011

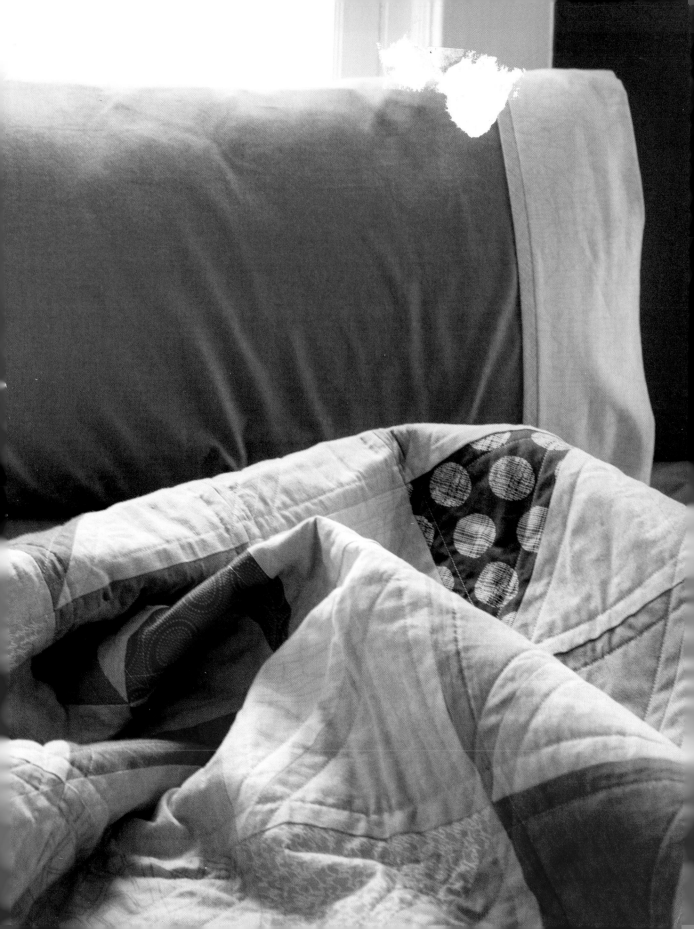

CONTENTS

ACKNOWLEDGMENTS

The phrase "it takes a village" comes to mind when thinking of the companies that provided products for this book: Clover notions, Pellon interfacing and batting, Olfa cutting supplies, Aurifil thread, and Janome sewing machines. Thanks to In the Beginning Fabrics Modern Solids and Robert Kaufman Fabrics for providing such gorgeous fabrics. These manufacturers produce products I have loved and used for years, and I am incredibly thankful for their assistance with this book.

Infinite gratitude to Sarah, Teressa, and the crew at Sarah's Fabrics in Lawrence, Kansas. There could not be a more perfect, beautiful, and inspiring photo shoot location!

Rae Ann Spitzenberger, your work continually left me speechless. I could not be more appreciative of your beautiful design.

My editors, your careful and attentive editing eyes made this book read exactly as I had envisioned.

Lauren Hunt, you made absolute magic happen with your camera and lenses. Including you was a no-brainer for me, and I will forever be thankful for your gorgeous photography and creative mind. Above all, though, I am thankful for our friendship.

Susanne Woods, thank you for your genuine excitement, for truly listening, and for starting something I couldn't wait to be a part of. Lucky Spool is one incredible company and I am deeply grateful for this opportunity.

DEDICATION

My parents: for your unwavering support and for the example you set. Dad, from you I learned the importance of craftsmanship and service to others. Mom, your presence as the School of Sewing teacher's aide was great for the students, but I value that time together more than you know. Thanks for teaching a young girl to sew all those years ago.

My husband, Richie: for celebrating this book from conception to completion, and for giving me my first sewing machine years ago so I could quit "borrowing" my mom's. I admire everything about you. X+1, right?

Our children: Eleanor, Graham, and Rhett. You are young, so I hope you won't remember the long hours mommy spent writing this book! However, I do hope you know how much of my sewing is inspired by and crafted just for you. Seeing you sit at your kid-size sewing machine with excitement and a "no fear" attitude brings me immense joy!

Bonnie Fish, my own favorite educator: for inscribing so long ago in my high school yearbook that I would one day write a book. You were right. I did it! Every student — sewing or otherwise — should have a cheerleader like you.

And last, but certainly not least: the School of Sewing "girls." There aren't adequate words to describe how proud I am of you all and how thankful I am that I was able to help guide you in your first year of sewing. We laughed, and we cried, and we sewed. Your enthusiasm for this project kept me going more than you know. That strangers became friends is probably my favorite part of our group. Here's to year two of The Feed Dogs!

THE CLASSROOM

A History Lesson

▶ The Origin of Our School of Sewing

Countless times I've heard friends say, "I have a sewing machine. I just don't know how to use it." That statement is typically followed by "Could you teach me?" One day, I had heard that question enough times to know I needed to do something about it. If my friends were serious about wanting to learn, I was serious about wanting to teach them. And just like that, our School of Sewing was born.

These students are my neighbors, former coworkers, fellow preschool moms, and childhood friends. Few of them knew another person in the group, but after one class, they were chatting like old friends. My own mother, who taught me to sew, even joined us as my teacher's aide! Their reasons for wanting to learn are varied, and their experience (or lack thereof) is typical of just about every beginner sewist out there. I hope that you relate to them and identify with their commentary throughout the book.

What you see here, within the pages and images in this book, is completely authentic. They are real women, who genuinely didn't know how to sew. Outside of very brief school projects as teenagers, they were total beginners. They needed help learning how to wind a bobbin, thread a machine, and fix a poorly sewn seam. Their quotes follow our full year of sewing together. Once the book entered the story line, I told my Publisher, Susanne, that my first priority was keeping the time line and curriculum unchanged, and making these women a huge part of this book. Luckily, she wholeheartedly agreed.

Gathering once a month, we worked for three or four hours at a time crafting small and practical projects, building skills and confidence levels, and leaving each class with a finished project in hand. Over the course of the year, word about our group quickly spread and I found myself having to turn away many who were interested in joining. My hope is that this book will inspire you to find a group, gather and create your own community, suggest a class to a local shop, or set your own pace. And see just how far sewing can take you.

Meet the Teacher

MY SEWING STORY

I love to sew. Enormous, fanatical, wild-about-it love. Mention the words "fabric" or "sewing" around me and I'll rattle on until you wish you hadn't brought it up. I'll stitch up just about anything: quilts, small gifts, bags, home decor, Halloween costumes, and clothes for my kids. I relish the chance to say, "Hey, look! I made this!" In my opinion, nothing beats the gift of handmade.

Ask many people and they'll likely remember the first (and probably only) thing they ever sewed. For me, it was a patchwork pillow in Mrs. Williams' middle school home economics class. A pillow that I still possess.

Other lessons in sewing have come along the way via books, YouTube, and tips from friends. But nothing beat learning from the women in my life. My mom taught me bit by bit whenever I expressed interest, project by project on her trusty machine. She tried, quite earnestly, to impress upon me the importance of proper pressing (sorry I didn't listen to that in those early days, Mom!). One of my grandmothers secretly helped me make my first quilt — a Christmas gift for my parents. I was sixteen and I remember proudly anticipating the moment they opened the box.

Even today, some of my most joyful moments are showing my children something new that I have sewn for them. When I hear my daughter Eleanor's excitement and see light in her eyes when she tells someone, "My mommy made my dress for me!" I could positively burst. Our son Graham got a massive thrill from sewing a simple pillow for his beloved stuffed dog. My children are learning the art of sewing from me, much like I learned from my own mother. However, a great many who wish to learn to sew don't have someone close to them who can teach them, as was the case for some of the women in our School of Sewing.

Once upon a time, I was a middle school math teacher. Today, I produce sewing patterns under the name Empty Bobbin Sewing Studio. Even with the fun I was having with my kids and business, I missed teaching and the personal interactions that come along with it. I missed the planning, and the predicting-what-students-need, and the advice-giving, and the encouraging. School of Sewing was the perfect storm: the desire and excitement from both teacher and student, a sewing curriculum based on achievable and usable projects, and the commitment to working together for a year. Each time one of my students learned a new sewing trick and reacted with wide eyes and excitement, my energy was renewed and my heart was full.

That wide-eyed excitement and potential is what I wish for you as you work through this book.

Welcome to class!

Meet the Students

▶ The School of Sewing Class Roster

MORGAN

I'm a new mother, living with my husband on a cattle farm in the small town where I grew up. All of this after years of living in the "big city," living an exciting life as an event planner, all the while admiring my best friend Shea's awesome sewing creations. I'm still learning, but with every cut and stitch I find more and more confidence.

Why I Wanted to Learn to Sew: For years, I witnessed my best friend make quilts for people, and even received one of them myself. I wanted to be able to participate in gifting something I made.

Proudest Moment: Putting a zipper in. I brag about it to my non-sewing friends!

Biggest Fear: Since I can't draw a straight line with a ruler, I was super afraid of cutting fabric. However, as with many things, practice does make perfect...or as close to perfect as I can get.

Best Piece of Advice: Just breathe. Oh, and measure twice!

AMY

My husband, Dan, and I have two young boys. I stay at home with them and have found myself busier than ever. I enjoy watching University of Kansas basketball (my alma mater!), traveling, spending time with family, and friends, and relaxing at the Lake of the Ozarks in the summer.

Biggest Fear: I worried that I would mess something up early on and not realize it until the end (and have to start all over again).

Proudest Moment: When we completed our pillowcase for the first project. Even though it was simple, it was exciting to realize that I could do this.

Favorite Sewing Tool: The seam guide is definitely one of my favorite tools. It makes sewing consistent seams so much easier and I love that it helps make the project look so professional.

Favorite Fabric: I don't have one specific favorite fabric, but I really like to find distinctive prints. I love having the opportunity to make something that exists in my mind, but that I haven't found in a store.

Best Piece of Advice: At some point you are going to mess something up and that is okay. You will get better as you gain more confidence and skill.

Front row, L to R: Mary, Mimi, Pam, Christine, Cheryl. Back row: Shea, Whitney, Amy, Cali, Morgan.

(literally) through the whole project and was so happy with what I made.

Favorite Fabric: If I'm being honest here, I like anything solid or with a random print on it because then I can't judge myself too harshly for not sewing straight.

Best Advice: Pressing well matters. Take it slowly. Peanut butter M&M's are the lifeblood of any successful, modern sewist.

CHERYL

I am a former third grade teacher and now a stay-at-home mom. Raising three young children with my husband, Brian, definitely keeps us entertained and on our toes. Between chasing a little one, shuffling to sports practices, and juggling school activities, I try my best to find a little "me time" by running and reading.

Biggest Fear: I had to get over the fear of my projects not turning out "right." I learned that when creating something by hand, the imperfections are what make it perfectly unique.

Proudest Moment: The first time I had to do "homework" on my own. When I completed it, I was so proud of myself. Well, I called Shea a few times with questions, but in the end I did it on my own.

Favorite School of Sewing Project: Hands down my favorite project was the tote bag. It was so much simpler than I originally thought. Friends can't believe that I made it!

Favorite Sewing Tool: The buttonhole foot. I was amazed how the machine just does it for you. Just push the pedal and BAM! it's done.

WHITNEY

I'm just a small-town girl on a quest for domestication! I met my prince charming and partner in crime, Evan, while studying broadcasting at BYU-Idaho. I am the lucky mom to two adorable children. I love all things girly — from Pinterest projects and decorating to School of Sewing, I try to bring a little creativity into my life while sweeping up cereal or singing Disney tunes with the kiddos.

Biggest Fear: Oh, how cutting terrified me. The majority of the time I cut fabric, I'd call my dear husband in for backup. "Measure twice, cut once," right?

Proudest Moment: Anything involving a zipper. I don't hyperventilate anymore when a project involves a zipper!

First Ever Sewing Project: We sewed sock monkeys in eighth grade. Pretty sure mine ended up looking like a dog...or bear... or fish. Basically anything but a monkey.

Favorite Sewing Tool: The walking foot. I also love how easy it is to use the guide bar for quilting evenly spaced lines!

Best Piece of Advice: Get an expert to lead you, guide you, walk beside you! I knew I wouldn't mess anything up too badly as long as my teacher was just a few feet away.

PAM

I spend my days in the classroom with energetic eighth graders and my nights at home with my awesome husband and dog. My life would be complete with a personal jet, a masseuse on-call, and a proposal from Jimmy Fallon and/or Brian Williams, but I'd settle for a night of eating out at a fun restaurant and a great live concert.

Biggest Fear: I was nervous that I might get excited about starting a new hobby and then ditch it after two months like I had done with all my other craft endeavors. I wanted to stick with it.

Proudest Moment: Without a doubt, I was thrilled with myself after making my tote bag. It was one of those situations where I didn't want to turn my bag right side out at the end because I was too nervous to see my final product. I was sweating

CHRISTINE

A self-proclaimed "sneaky chef," I enjoy finding new ways to feed healthy meals to my husband and two young children. During the day, I'm a special services teacher and autism consultant for the local school district, and my evenings are usually spent running between the kids' various activities. I've really enjoyed my newfound sewing hobby, and have embraced it as what I know will become a lifelong activity!

Why I Wanted to Learn to Sew: I wanted to create meaningful gifts for my family and friends. I started looking on Pinterest and Shea's blog, wishing I could make some of those fun projects. A gift is much more enjoyable to give when you make it yourself.

Biggest Fear: Making a mistake! I spend a ton of time looking for that perfect fabric, so I don't want to make an error when cutting or sewing my project.

Proudest Moment: Learning to sew a zipper. I carried that zippered pillow cover everywhere just to say, "Hey, look what I made!"

Favorite Sewing Tool: My great big 24″ x 36″ cutting mat is by far my favorite!

Best Piece of Advice: Be patient and find a good mentor.

CALI

I am a middle school English teacher, working mostly with gifted students. When I'm not working with hormonal middle schoolers, I'm playing with our twin toddlers. There isn't a huge difference...trust me. I love to read, travel, cook, and sew. I drink entirely too much Diet Coke, my floors are rarely clean, and our children eat more goldfish crackers than vegetables. But we always have a good time!

First Ever Sewing Project: It was 1987. Seventh grade home ec class. I made a bag with Mickey Mouse fabric and a big red button on the front. And I still have it.

Favorite School of Sewing Project: I LOVE the tote bag. I've now made so many that I no longer need the directions.

Favorite Fabric: Basically, I love everything Anna Maria Horner designs. I love big designs and bold patterns.

Favorite Sewing Tool: I love my Olfa cutting mat. And my flower head pins.

Best Piece of Advice: Don't be afraid! It is such a great feeling to watch a project go from just a stack of cool fabric to an actual, usable product. Start small. Start with something you can do in one sitting. The feeling of accomplishment is fantastic!

MIMI

I am a wife, mother, and want-to-be runner. I work full-time for a large global banking institution in the information technology department. I have two wonderful kids, and a fantastic husband who has supported me during my learning-to-sew phase!

Biggest Fear: Picking out great-looking fabric combinations. Finding fabrics that complement each other can be so tricky!

Proudest Moment: When I figured out the rotary cutter and was able to feel confident about cutting my own fabric.

Favorite Fabric: Anything black and white. That matches everything! I have trouble dressing myself, let alone picking out the perfect fabrics to go together!

Favorite School of Sewing Project: The apron!

Favorite Sewing Tool: My lovely seam ripper. It is used frequently. And my iron. My love for ironing runs quite deep.

Meet the Reader

▸ You and Why You're Here

Chances are you're holding this book for one of two reasons:

▸ You want to learn to sew.

▸ You want to teach someone to sew.

We'll get to those details in the next chapter, but for now, let's talk about sewing and the amazing resurgence the craft is experiencing.

THE RETURN OF SEWING

In my mother's and grandmother's generations, sewing your own clothing made sense from an economic standpoint. It was less costly to buy fabric and make a dress than to buy one from a store. Today, the opposite is true. I could buy a Christmas dress for my daughter for far less than the cost of the fabric and pattern. (But year after year, I make dresses for her birthday and Christmas!) Because of this shift, many eschewed their sewing machines and the craft took a hit. Sure, some people have always been sewing, but the fact remains that fewer people were sewing and far fewer were passing on or being taught this wonderfully important and useful skill. Thankfully, people are regaining a much greater appreciation for handmade these days. One need look no further than Etsy, home to hundreds of thousands of sellers sharing their handmade wares. And thanks to Pinterest boards, we have a way to organize, clip, and gather both inspiration and projects to our little DIY heart's content.

Sewing is cool again and I, for one, couldn't be happier.

THE NEW FACE OF LEARNING

Many of the projects we see in online handmade shops and photo-sharing sites have passed through a sewing machine at one point. Those who grew up not learning to sew are eager to master the art of needle and thread and are seeking lessons, tutorials, classes, and tips to make their sewing machines hum. Learning takes place in so many new forms now — online videos and tutorials, blogs, e-books, and online classes. This new face of learning is amazing; the whole world is literally in the palm of your hand, one click or finger tap away. Having said that, there is something reassuring about having someone right by your side to provide in-person help and feedback that makes each new skill really sink in when you're learning to sew. Whether you plan to be the teacher or the student, having another person sitting right next to you is irreplaceable.

WHY YOU'RE HERE

You're here holding this copy of *School of Sewing*. What do you want to make the most? Whom do you want to bestow your handmade gifts upon? If you're using this book as a teaching tool, what essentials do you want your students to gain and learn? As you work through this book, keep those things in mind, because next we're going to dive in and talk about forming your own sewing community — whether you're the teacher or the student. If you don't know where to start, you're going to love the next chapter!

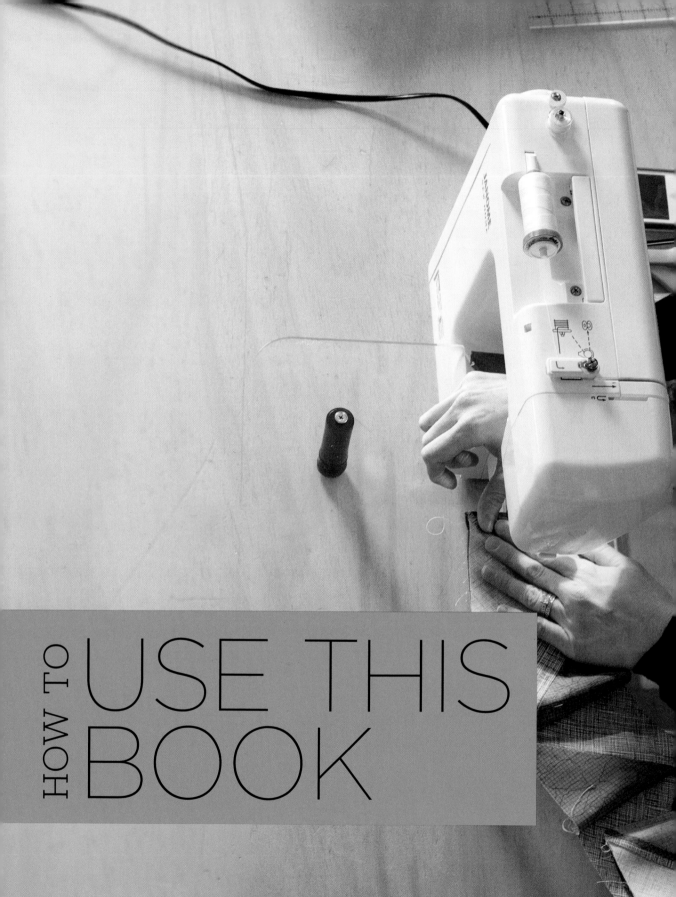

HOW TO USE THIS BOOK

Learn It

▶ Teach Yourself to Sew

If you picked up this book because you want to learn to sew, give yourself a high five and pat yourself on the back. Welcome to the wonderful world of sewing! I have included all of the details, tips, and tricks that our own School of Sewing students needed most. You'll also find intermediate skills covered in the form of easy-to-find "Extra Credit" built into each project. A few things to keep in mind as you learn with this book:

BUDDY UP

This is my biggest piece of advice when it comes to teaching yourself. Find a friend who wants to sew, share your successes or struggles, and answer each other's questions as you work your way through the book together. Plus, you can share supplies! If you don't have a specific person teaching you from the book, ask your circle of family and friends.

Perhaps someone could become a mentor of sorts, offer advice via phone and maybe even an in-person session or two. Put out the call in your social media circles and you might be surprised by who comes out of the woodwork to join you.

ADD SUPPLIES GRADUALLY

In our group and in this book, we progress through our projects in a way that allows supplies to build up over time. Buying supplies all at once may not fit into your budget. Borrow whenever you can first and decide if you like a brand or model. When you're ready to buy, you can refer to the specific supplies I've recommended throughout. For detailed summaries of brands I believe are worthy of your cash, see School Supplies (page 32).

THE BOOK STRUCTURE

While the projects can be made in any order, they are arranged to allow for the gradual addition of terms, skills, and supplies. I suggest reading Driver's Ed (page 52), before you start sewing,

and again as you work through the projects. Tips and steps that weren't clear before you'd sewn anything will suddenly make sense and you can begin to implement the techniques as needed. The Help Desk (page 68) is one to bookmark for sure. Speaking of troubleshooting, our School of Sewing class worked hard to think of all the possible project-specific tricky spots that we encountered. Advice on how to deal with these are woven into the project instructions themselves.

THE STUDENT QUOTES

I think that you will identify with the students profiled here. They have so much to share — insights, tips, proud moments, and hilarious moments of tangled threads and seam-ripping sessions. They began right where you are. I wish you could have been with us on the night of our first class and again for our final quilt session at the end of our year. You'd see the amazing growth, knowledge, and confidence that comes from regular sewing sessions. Remember, no one learns this stuff overnight. It takes time. Think of the mistakes as learning opportunities. They're good for you. Promise.

Teach It

▶ **Using the Book as a Teaching Tool**

THINK ABOUT GROUP SIZE

This is a big one. You want to help bring people into the world of sewing, but in order to do it well, you need to manage the size of your group. I taught eight. Eight is a lot for a single person to teach outside of a local fabric shop class, especially if they are true beginners. Having my mom as my teacher's aide was essential given our group size. The more true beginners you have, the smaller your group should be. Sewing one-on-one with a good friend can be extremely rewarding and you can customize the speed of your lessons more easily. Don't stress if the people in your group do not already know each other — my group was made up of strangers, and I adore the close community we've become because of the class.

FIND A LOCATION

This, of course, depends upon the size of your group. A kitchen or basement space could work for a smaller group. If you have a local fabric store, ask if they would be interested in starting up a School of Sewing monthly group! We do not have a fabric store nearby, and we quickly outgrew my kitchen. After looking around, we secured a community clubhouse. Check with local churches, libraries, and even community centers. You might be surprised by what they can offer. The main factors to consider are decent lighting and adequate table space for machines and cutting.

FIND A DATE

Perhaps the trickiest part of all. Like most of us, my group had extremely busy family schedules. In order to work around jobs, travel, family, and other obligations, we found that a free online group scheduling tool made it very fast and easy to find nights that worked best. We used Doodle.com and I highly recommend it!

GEAR UP

I created a School of Sewing tub that traveled to class with me each month. I kept extension cords, surge bars, a radio to spin some tunes, and a box of basic sewing supplies in case someone forgot something. I also threw in my spool rack so that my class could use a specific color of thread. A thread stash is often the last thing on new sewists' lists. Paper bags make great individual trash cans, so I always had those in the tub, too. A couple students brought irons and ironing boards to class each time, and my mom brought some desk lamps. It really did take a village, but we had our own system and it just trucked along, month after month. Oh, and packing snacks is wise, too!

ASSIGN HOMEWORK

At first, we did everything together from start to finish. For the first class, I cut the pillowcase pieces ahead of time and let the students pick out a "pillowcase kit" when they arrived. We didn't even touch cutting tools or even talk about them until the second class. This allowed us to focus on talking about the basics and get sewing. Leaving class with a finished project was essential to the success of our group. Gradually, I had students do any cutting and fusing of interfacing prior to class. This allowed us to finish a project in a single three- to four-hour class (with the exception of the quilt).

"Each month, I went home and made the project again within a few days of class. It helped to get the skills to sink in and really built my confidence. I could do it on my own!" —MIMI

AWARD PRIZES

This was always fun for me. I tried to have a fun item to give away each class. A seam ripper was awarded to the first person to need one. A small pack of Clover Wonder Clips was given to the student who asked the most questions. I shopped my stash for duplicates or bought inexpensive but useful notions. When you're starting from scratch, a simple gifted $3 seam ripper goes a long way.

PUT YOURSELF IN THEIR SHOES

This is essential for a successful group. At our first class, I emphasized that students should harness their nervousness and turn it into a question-

asking, seam-ripper-embracing, no-fear approach to sewing. I said the same thing I used to tell my seventh grade math students: "No one's going to laugh if you ask a 'stupid question.' They're going to be *relieved* that you asked. You'll be the hero." Learning something new can be nerve-wracking, especially as an adult. Commiserate over the tangled bobbin mess and celebrate the perfectly topstitched curve. You'll build a supportive and inviting community before you know it.

This Book

WHAT IT IS

▸ Written with the true beginner in mind. I worked hard not to assume too much prior knowledge.

▸ Built-in terminology, right when you need it. Terms are introduced in order of appearance and also included in the glossary and index.

▸ Small, functional projects that can be completed in one class. (Except for the quilt. That one takes a few classes!)

▸ Projects to make for gifts or for yourself. I drafted the project list with input from my students. Gifts were at the top of the list.

▸ A set of basic skills, gradually built over the course of the book. Techniques are repeated in projects to show use in a variety of situations and to offer more chance for practice.

▸ Like a friend is sitting next to you, predicting the trouble spots and helping you to problem solve.

WHAT IT ISN'T

▸ Clothing, baby projects, or items for pets. I looked at the projects that the students in my class wanted to make and crafted a sewing curriculum with broad appeal. We included projects that anyone could use, regardless of clothing size or pet/kid status. If you want to sew clothing (and I think you should!), look for some suggested titles in the Resources section on page 158.

▸ Complicated. I wanted students to walk out of every class with a finished "Hey! Look what I made!" project.

▸ A be-all, end-all set of sewing skills. Are there skills I'm not including here? Definitely. There's room to grow, but with a solid foundation.

▸ For all fabric types. I wanted my students to sew with fabrics that were easy to source and easiest to use, both in sewing and in daily wear and tear. Specialty fabrics can be amazing, but they often require special needles and stitches. For our year together, we focused on commonly found quilting cotton and home decor weight fabrics. We'll go into more detail on fabrics on page 43.

My Hope for You

Before we jump into the sewing, I encourage you to seek the following goals as you use this book:

GIVE THE GIFT OF HANDMADE

Give a gift of gratitude or appreciation to a teacher or neighbor. Welcome a new life. Celebrate a marriage. Comfort friends who have experienced a loss. Simple or elaborate, making your gift will give you more in return than you can imagine.

LEARN SOMETHING NEW

Learning is always in style, especially when it's something tangible you can show others! For an added wrinkle-in-the-brain bonus, challenge yourself with the Extra Credit options for each project. These suggest more intermediate techniques to really stretch your newly acquired skills.

BUILD A COMMUNITY

Be it a community of two or five or ten, I wish for you the laughter and camaraderie that we experienced in our School of Sewing.

REMEMBER TO SHARE

And please share your stories with me! Use the hashtag #SchoolofSewing on social media sites such as Instagram, Facebook, and Twitter. The night of our very first class, before the book was even a thought in my mind, I posted a photo on Instagram of my eight friends, gathered to sew in my kitchen. A slew of encouraging comments came in from around the globe, and ever since then I have been sharing images here and there from our sessions together. The more we share and tag images of our #SchoolofSewing moments, the more we can learn from and encourage each other — celebrating finished projects and giving a virtual nod of understanding for those seam-ripper moments.

YOUR SEWING MACHINE

Types of Machines

▶ Decisions, Decisions, Decisions

Shopping for a sewing machine involves comparing features and prices, but for the new sewist it is first important to note the differences between the three types of sewing machines available.

MECHANICAL

These straightforward machines have all the basic stitches you need to sew: straight and zigzag stitches and a buttonhole. Dials are used to select from a set of stitches, stitch widths, and lengths. Because of this, there is slightly less precision control over your stitches. Older mechanical machines made from metal housing can often be found on the secondary market. Typically, a secondary market machine will be a less expensive option, unless you find an all-metal machine. I learned to sew on my mother's all-metal mechanical 1980s Bernina, which she still owns. It is a steady workhorse! Industrial sewing machines are popular among sewists who want a dependable, long-lasting machine for straight stitches only.

ELECTRONIC

Electronic models are easy to spot with their lit-up screens on the front of the housing. Buttons are used to select stitches and set the length, width, and tension with precision, while sliders are used for speed control. A variety of buttonhole styles are usually available, and these machines typically offer decorative stitches or small letters, if those options appeal to you.

COMPUTERIZED

The most expensive and elaborate machines in the lineup. Computerized machines can typically be spotted by their large screens and higher price tags. Many even feature a touch screen or come with embroidery attachments to create intricate designs. Some of these machines actually connect to your computer or tablet device.

COMPUTERIZED

ELECTRONIC

MECHANICAL

Anatomy of a Sewing Machine

▶ A Tour of Dials, Levers, and Buttons

While each manufacturer and model is unique, there are a basic set of parts present on most sewing machines. If you already own one, sit down with your machine and its manual and work your way through these diagrams. Eventually, you'll start referring to the "handwheel" and the "feed dogs" instead of calling them the "thingamajigs." In the meantime, mark this page so you can refer to it as often as needed. Follow along in order and you'll have completed a great tour of your machine and understand what makes it tick. Remember, your machine might not have every feature you see here on the Janome Magnolia 7330. If you are looking to buy your first machine, you'll find buying tips in on page 29.

BASICS

❶ **Power switch:** Much like a computer, your machine won't work if it is not turned on!

❷ **Power jack:** You'll plug your power cord in here.

❸ **Foot pedal:** The gas pedal for your machine. Press it lightly or put the pedal to the metal. It controls your sewing speed. Some machines have a start/stop button in addition to the foot pedal.

❹ **Presser foot:** The leading lady in the whole show! Most of your attention will be focused here while you're sewing. Shaped like an L, the presser foot holds the fabric in place. Many different feet are available for virtually all sewing tasks, but you'll only need a few for the projects in this book. We'll get to more details on the differences between presser feet on page 27.

❺ **Presser foot lever:** Raises and lowers the presser foot. Find your lever on either the back of the machine or the inside of the machine arm. Many machines allow you to raise it even higher than the standard raised position. I call it the "super lift" and use this when positioning my presser foot over extra-thick fabrics and seams.

THREADING AND WINDING

⑥ Handwheel: While you're sewing away, this wheel is turning. You can also manually turn the wheel to raise and lower the presser foot, a move that is particularly useful when sewing over unusually thick seams or when pivoting at corners. On many mechanical machines, you will pull out on the handwheel to disengage the machine so that you can wind a bobbin. The handwheel is also often called a flywheel.

⑦ Spool pins: These hold your spool of thread while you sew. If your machine has a spool pin cap, use it on top of your thread to keep it from hopping around while you sew. Some machines have both a horizontal and a vertical spool pin. Use a vertical spool pin for threads wound in a straight pattern and a horizontal spool pin for threads woven in a crisscross pattern.

⑧ Thread guides: These position and guide the thread through the machine. Refer to your manual and follow the directions carefully. Don't skip even one of these thread guides! I can't stress this enough. Each one is vital to proper thread tension while you sew.

⑨ Thread tension discs: Hidden within your machine, this mechanism controls how much thread passes through the thread path on the way to the needle. When you pull the thread down and under in a U shape and back up to the take-up lever, you've guided the thread into these discs inside your machine.

⑩ Take-up lever: This looks like a gooseneck and when you turn the handwheel, you'll notice that it moves up and down with the needle. With each movement, it pulls just the right amount of thread for the stitch.

⑪ Bobbin winder/bobbin winder stop: This holds the bobbin for winding/refilling. Depending on your machine, you'll either slide the bobbin over to the stop or move the stop toward the bobbin.

⑫ Bobbin winding tension disc: This round knob is actually a tension disc that controls the thread as it comes off the spool and fills the empty bobbin. An improperly or loosely wound bobbin (page 54) can usually be traced back to thread not making it into this tension disc. Each machine is different and you'll want to wind thread around it correctly, so use your manual.

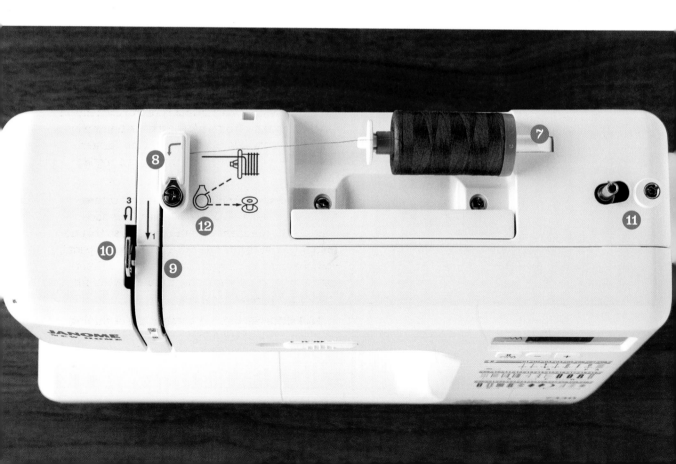

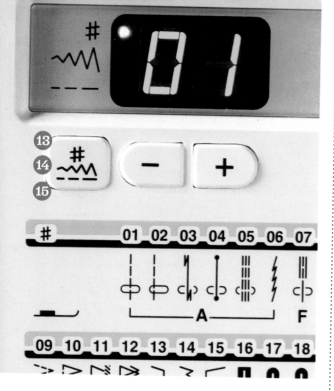

STITCHES

⑬ Stitch selector: Most often used will be a straight stitch and a zigzag, but your machine may offer an array of decorative stitches, too.

⑭ Stitch width selector: Control how far to the left and right a stitch goes. This is vital when sewing a zigzag or when positioning your needle to the left or right for topstitching

⑮ Stitch length selector: Control how long your stitches are by using this feature, which determines how much fabric is fed under the needle between stitches.

STITCH CONTROLS

⑯ Reverse button/lever: Used for — you guessed it! — sewing in reverse or sewing a backstitch. Some machines feature a button and others require raising or pressing a lever.

⑰ Needle up/down: An ultra-handy feature that comes on some models. When engaged, this feature means that the needle will remain down when you stop sewing. Whether you're pivoting at a corner or stopping to reposition your hands, your needle will keep the fabric from shifting. Don't underestimate how amazing this feature is. If you've got it, use it!

⑱ Thread tension selector/dial: Control the tension disc settings with this dial. Loosen the tension by turning it to the left or a lower number. Tighten the tension by turning it to the right or a higher number.

⑲ Speed control: Another nice-to-have feature that is not standard on all machines. This slider controls the top speed of your machine, so that no matter how hard you press down on the foot pedal, your machine won't speed away from you. Great for sewing carefully around curves. Excellent for teaching children to sew, too!

⑳ Lockstitch: Secures the stitch at the beginning or end of a line of stitching.

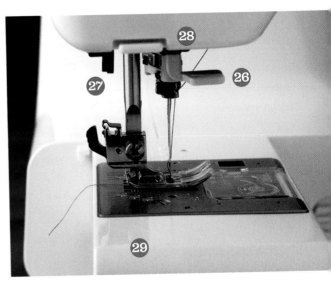

NEEDLE AND BOBBIN

㉑ Bobbin case/housing: The bobbin sits here, providing the thread for the bottom stitches. Your machine may have a see-through bobbin case or a removable metal case. These differences are covered in detail on page 54. There is a specific direction that the bobbin should be threaded and placed inside the case, so be sure you check your manual. Those thread directions matter!

㉒ Throat plate: This flat plate protects the gears while leaving the feed dogs exposed. There are grooves for a variety of seam allowances marked. These are measured from the needle's center position. This can also be called a needle plate.

㉓ Feed dogs: These feed the fabric through the machine. Tiny teeth lightly grab the fabric and pull it to the back at a speed controlled by how hard you press the foot pedal down. Without using fabric or thread, press on the foot pedal for a close-up view of the feed dogs in action. No need for you to shove the fabric through — just do a little steering! On some machines, you can lower the feed dogs, which is useful for free motion quilting.

㉔ Needle: Your needle is a VIP for your sewing, so study it carefully. It is inserted into the needle bar and held in place with a screw. Take a quick peek at the top of the needle bar and you'll notice a thread guide that many often miss. Look for a small hook or bar to slide thread behind before bringing the thread down to the eye of the needle.

㉕ Needle screw: Use this to tighten or change your needle, which should be done after every major project.

㉖ Needle threader: More and more new machines are made with this handy feature. If your machine has a needle threader, take the time to read your manual and learn the specifics for your model. It will save you from squinting to poke the end of your thread through the eye of the needle.

㉗ One-step buttonhole lever: If your machine sews a one-step buttonhole, you'll lower this for use in conjunction with your buttonhole foot (page 27).

㉘ Thread cutter: No need to grab your scissors after each pass through the machine. Just raise your presser foot, pull the fabric to the side, and run the thread tails through this blade to cut the threads. You can always trim more closely later. Some higher end machines feature an automatic thread cutter that trims your thread close to the fabric with the push of a button. Yes, it is as awesome as it sounds.

㉙ Free arm: Most machines feature a removable accessory box to allow for the sewing of small or narrow projects, such as sleeves. Depending upon your bobbin style, you may need to expose the free arm of your machine in order to replace the bobbin.

Presser Feet Primer

Knowing which presser foot to use for your specific project can greatly improve your results. Along with properly pressing your fabric, using the right presser foot is one of the best ways to achieve a professional finish on your project. The presser feet available extend far beyond this list, so keep your eyes open for options made for your machine and for the type of sewing you do most often.

The appearance and method of attaching feet vary from machine to machine. Glancing at presser feet from above shows obvious differences, but don't forget the underneath of each foot, which makes a difference in how the fabric and stitches feed through the machine. Most newer machines feature snap-on presser feet, where the individual feet snap on to a shank or bar that is screwed onto the presser bar. Other machines, specifically mechanical machines, feature screw-on feet. These feet are removed and replaced by loosening and tightening a screw.

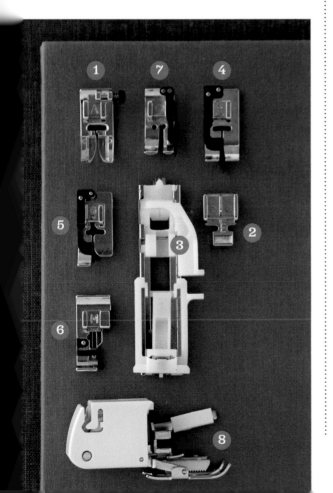

ESSENTIAL FEET

1. **All-purpose/zigzag foot:** This foot comes standard with all machines and is the foot you will use most often. The wide opening allows you to position the needle to the left or right in order to sew zigzag stitches.

2. **Zipper foot:** Another foot that comes standard with most machines. The design of this foot allows the needle to sew right along the zipper teeth.

3. **Buttonhole foot:** This odd-looking foot is actually an amazing tool, so don't avoid it simply because of its appearance. This foot will automatically sew buttonholes, with most machines sewing a buttonhole up to 1" in length. To use it, you insert the button into a slot in the back of the foot, which determines the size of the buttonhole. You'll make a buttonhole for Project 6, the Tech Case.

NICE-TO-HAVE FEET

4. **Ditch or edgestitch foot:** The guide at the center of this foot helps you follow and stitch in or near a seam line. I like to position my needle to the left and use this foot for topstitching. With my fabric edge or seam against the guide, I can sew topstitching at a perfectly consistent distance from the seam.

5. **Blind hem foot:** Use this foot to create invisible hems on items such as garments or curtains. The guide keeps stitches lined up with a fabric's folded edge.

6. **Overcasting foot:** If you plan to sew with knit fabric, this foot will be handy. The guide in the center holds your fabric edge flat and in place, allowing a zigzag stitch to cover the raw edge.

7. **Quarter-inch foot:** Another foot with a handy guide! This foot is perfect for piecing quilt tops, or making doll clothes, or any other project where a ¼" seam allowance is key. I use mine daily!

8. **Walking foot:** Quilters can't live without this one, because it is especially useful for sewing thick layers. The walking foot grips and pulls fabric from the top while the machine's feed dogs pull fabric from below, allowing both layers to move under the needle at the same rate, preventing puckers.

SPECIALTY FEET

⑨ Rolled hem foot: This foot comes in a variety of sizes for different hem widths. Fabric is fed through the opening on this foot. As you sew the foot folds the raw edge over twice, completely encasing the raw edge.

⑩ Ruffler foot: The appearance of this foot might take you by surprise (and the rhythmic clunking sound it makes as it works might do the same!), but this foot can be a lifesaver if you are sewing yards of fabric into a ruffle or a pleat. The foot creates pleats as fabric is fed through.

⑪ Free motion quilting foot: When you think of sewing, you likely think of a straight stitch sewn as fabric passes through the machine. A free motion foot allows you to sew in any direction and is often used to create quilting designs, such as loops and swirls. Lowering the feed dogs is essential when using this foot.

⑫ Button foot: A miracle of modern sewing! Sew a two or four-hole button to your project with this foot, using a zigzag stitch and stitch length of zero. Try it and be amazed!

⑬ Appliqué foot: At first glance, it just looks like a regular foot, but the wide groove found on the bottom of this foot makes extra room for thick decorative stitches and appliqué projects. Sometimes it is referred to as an open-toe foot. (What's appliqué, you ask? See Appliqué 101, page 101.)

⑭ Roller foot: When sewing with fabrics such as vinyl or leather or another fabric that shifts or sticks easily, a roller foot can be very useful. The textured rollers on the foot provide the grip necessary to move the fabrics smoothly through the machine.

⑮ Invisible zipper foot: A specialty foot made specifically for invisible zippers. This foot allows zippers to be installed so that they are not seen from the outside of the project. It is also called a concealed zipper.

⑯ Gathering foot: This foot typically comes in a snap-on form. By adjusting the thread tension and stitch length, this foot allows you to add a gentle gather to your fabric.

⑰ Circular sewing attachment foot: The math class compass-loving nerd in you might really love how this foot works. Set a radius for your circle and a pin holds the fabric in place at the center while your machine sews a perfect circle. Can be used with a straight stitch or decorative stitches.

⑱ Cording and pintucking feet: Groves on the bottom of these feet keep trim or piping in place as you sew. The multiple grooves on the pintucking foot are smaller than on the cording foot (often called the piping foot), which has two larger grooves.

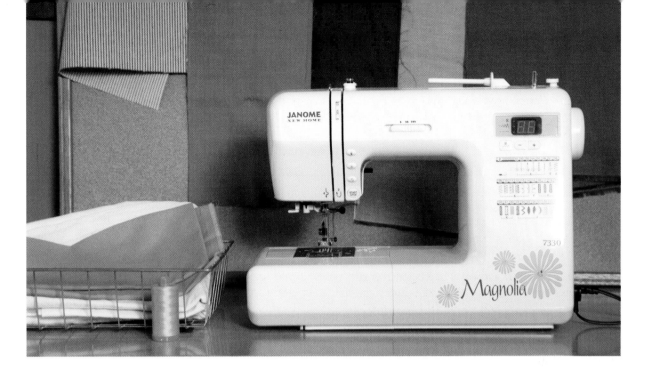

The Machine of Your Dreams

▶ What to Look For

Shopping for a machine can be overwhelming. But it certainly doesn't have to be that way. At its core, sewing is using thread and a needle to sew fabric together using a straight line. That is really all you need. However, we live in a world full of options. And, boy, do we love options! Based on my own experience and that of the women in the School of Sewing, I have classified features as "must-have," "nice-to-have," and "bonus". Like finding the right college or house (or even spouse!), you'll know in your gut it's the right one when you find it.

▶ **MACHINE-SPECIFIC REVIEWS**
There are numerous places to look for user reviews. Blog posts can be limited and hard to find, and Amazon.com does not sell every model from every manufacturer. I recommend the machine review section of PatternReview.com. Users post everything from price paid to pros and cons of specific machines. This is the place to go if you want real feedback from people about specific models. Keep in mind, though, that a review from another person should not take the place of a test drive on the machine yourself.

MUST-HAVE FEATURES

▶ **A GREAT STITCH:** A solid straight stitch with excellent thread tension is essential.

▶ **A STURDY BASE:** Does the machine bounce or move around when you sew? If you want perfectly straight stitches, you need a machine with a heavy base.

▶ **ADJUSTABLE NEEDLE POSITIONS:** Being able to adjust the needle from the center to the left or right is extremely useful for topstitching, sewing zippers, or achieving a specific seam allowance.

▶ **A FREE ARM:** Removing part of the base allows you to sew more easily in tighter spaces, like shirt sleeves or around the tops of tote bags.

NICE-TO-HAVE FEATURES

▶ **NEEDLE UP/DOWN:** When this feature is engaged, the needle remains down when you stop sewing. This means that when you pivot at a corner, a curve, or stop to reposition your hands, the fabric won't shift and the stitches will stay perfectly in line. See page 25.

▶ **DROP-IN BOBBIN:** I prefer these for a beginner simply for ease of use in winding and inserting and for the ability to easily see how much thread is left on the bobbin. See page 55.

▶ **ONE-STEP BUTTONHOLE:** Making a buttonhole in one step is far easier and faster than in a traditional but cumbersome four step method. Select the right setting, lower your presser foot, and instantly sew a buttonhole! See page 121.

▶ **BRIGHT LIGHT:** Unless you'll be sewing only on sunny days near big windows, you'll want a bright light to illuminate the needle/presser foot area.

AWESOME BONUS FEATURES

▶ **AUTOMATIC THREAD CUTTER:** Push a button and the machine trims the top and bottom thread close to your fabric. See page 26.

▶ **ADJUSTABLE SPEED CONTROL:** Controlling your speed by pressing less on the foot pedal is fine, but to really control the speed of your sewing, an adjustable slider is very useful. I use mine each time I sew a curve. This option is especially helpful if a child will be using your machine. See page 25.

▶ **NEEDLE THREADER:** Rather than squint and aim for the needle hole, you can use this mechanism to pull the thread through the hole. It's a feature I use each time I thread my needle. See page 26.

▶ **METAL PARTS:** Metal is simply more sturdy than plastic. Look for a machine with as many parts and pieces made from metal as possible. Keep in mind that many machines will have metal parts inside, but will be covered in a plastic housing. If you're unsure, ask the dealer.

Where to Buy

▶ New, Used, and Borrowed

The sewing machines of today are not what they were when your grandmother learned to sew, or even when your mother learned, which can be both good and bad. You'll see more plastic parts, but you'll also see more options and features. There isn't one magical machine that has every feature for an amazing low price. But hunting is half the fun, right?

FROM A LOCAL DEALER

Buying from a local dealer is my number-one recommendation. They know their machines inside and out and offer a full line of machines from basic to fancy computerized machines, sergers, and embroidery machines. Different dealers specialize in specific brands, so ask around and search manufacturer websites for dealers in your area. Buying a model on the lower end of the price range from a dealer might mean you can upgrade or use the same specialty attachments and accessories with a nicer machine from the same manufacturer down the road. Plus, many dealers offer free classes with the purchase of a machine or maintenance deals for the first year. Dealers also often offer pre-owned or trade-in machines for sale, which may be a great happy medium for you.

Each of the members of our School of Sewing used a Janome Magnolia 7330. I recommend it each time someone asks me about a great machine. Why? It's one of the most affordable machines for the features it includes. Needle up/down, needle threader, free arm, needle positioning, one-step buttonhole, speed control, and the optional extension table are the top features that we used regularly for the projects in this book.

ONLINE

If you don't have a local dealer for the machine you want, or if you don't have a local dealer at all, buying online may be the answer. However, if something goes wrong, you don't have a store to rely on for maintenance or classes, and some manufacturers do not sell their machines online or limit the models that are offered.

USED OR HAND-ME-DOWN

Buying used can be tricky. There are many people who buy expensive machines, only to find that sewing is not for them. These machines can be a great buy, but you should proceed with caution. If a machine has not been used in years (or even months) you have no guarantee that it really is in great working condition.

Hand-me-down machines or borrowing from someone can be a nice low-commitment option. If the machine has been gathering dust, I recommend having a sewing machine technician examine it before you buy or start sewing. If you can find a solid new-to-you machine that has been serviced and used regularly, you've got a winner!

SOME PARTING ADVICE

Avoid the basic models offered in chain stores. An $80 machine sounds like a fabulous idea, but if you experience problems, there is no store to back you with help, service, and classes.

Set a specific budget that you are comfortable with. It can be very easy to want more and more machine once you are looking at a whole line of them in a store. If the machine you want is out of your budget, look around your house. You might be able to do just what Cheryl did!

"I was ready to commit to sewing and purchase a machine, but it didn't feel right to go out and buy one right then and there. I decided to sell off some household things that were unused and collecting dust, so I pulled out an envelope and labeled it 'sewing machine money.' Several weeks later, I walked out of the dealer's door with a big brown box containing my brand-new sewing machine, and I didn't have to impact the family budget to get it!" —CHERYL

THE TEST DRIVE

Once you find a machine you think you want to buy, be sure to check out the following:

▶ What accessories and presser feet come with the machine?

▶ Watch it sew a buttonhole. Does the buttonhole look nice when finished?

▶ What if you want to upgrade in the future? Is there a trade-in program? Can you use your presser feet on that upgrade machine, too?

▶ How many layers can it sew? Try sewing on a variety of fabrics, including very thick layers like denim and home decor fabrics. You may need to change the needle for this part of the test. Examine both the topstitches and those on the underside of the project. Can it handle sewing four or six layers of fabric?

▶ How much noise does it make while sewing?

▶ Are classes and maintenance included with the purchase?

▶ Finally, be sure *you* are the one who is sitting at the machine and sewing during any test drive, rather than sitting next to the salesperson while they demonstrate.

SCHOOL SUPPLIES

Cutting Supplies

A professional, finished look to your project starts with accurate cutting. These are the tools I use and adore.

SHEARS

High-quality fabric scissors are essential for sewing. Never cut paper or other materials with them (and make sure everyone in your house knows this!). If there is one cutting tool I find indispensable, it is my pair of 8" Gingher knife-edge dressmaker shears. Mine are nearly a decade old — because the blades are steel, they can be sharpened from time to time and last a lifetime.

SNIPS

A small 4" pair of embroidery snips or scissors are used for trimming threads. The sharper the point, the closer you can get to the fabric, which will give a cleaner look to your projects.

CLEAR ACRYLIC RULERS

A perfectly straight cut is made easier with one of these. The ruler is clear, allowing you to see the fabric underneath, and marked in ⅛" intervals for accurate measuring. To start out, I recommend a 6" x 24" ruler to cut yardage across the entire width of fabric. Once you know what type of projects you'll make most, you can add to your ruler arsenal. A wide variety of square and rectangle dimensions are available, as well as other shapes such as triangles and trapezoids. Other favorites include 12" x 12", 2" x 12", and 9" x 9".

CUTTING MAT

A self-healing cutting mat is used with a rotary cutter and acrylic ruler. They come in many sizes, and I recommend buying the largest one you can afford. Mats smaller than 24" x 36" will mean you will have to reposition the fabric in order to make each cut. Each brand marks measurements along the outside in different ways, so choose the one that makes the most sense to you. I use a 24" x 36" Olfa mat, and it is the only mat I need.

Must-haves: 45-millimeter rotary cutter, the highest quality shears you can afford, snips, 6" x 24" acrylic ruler, the largest cutting mat you can afford, a basic seam ripper.

SEAM RIPPER

Un-sewing is just as important as sewing, and for that, you need a seam ripper. Mistakes happen but, thanks to this tool, they are surprisingly easy to fix.

ROTARY CUTTER

These are used to slice through multiple layers of fabric, cutting as the blade rolls along. Rotary cutters come in a variety of blade sizes, handle styles, and price points, with a 45-millimeter blade being the standard size. Blades with a smaller diameter are great for cutting curves, while 60-millimeter blades are great for slicing through thick projects with batting. Whatever size you choose, you'll want some replacement blades on hand, too.

▶ *See Glossary for pinking shears and paper scissors.*

Sewing Supplies

SEWING MACHINE NEEDLES

Not all needles are created equally. Needles come in a mind-boggling variety of sizes and styles, each suited to a different type of fabric and sewing, including double and triple, denim, ballpoint, universal, and more. Look closely at the top portion of the needle and you'll see that it is flat on one side and rounded on the other side for proper insertion into the machine. Needle sizes are classified by numbers: the larger the number the thicker and heavier the fabric it is meant to sew. For the projects in this book, we used universal, microtex/sharp, and denim needles. If you plan to sew knits, you'll need a ballpoint needle. I almost always have a Schmetz microtex needle in my machine.

MACHINE SEAM GUIDE

Sometimes called a cloth guide, this acts like a guardrail of sorts, keeping your fabric at a consistent distance from the needle for an accurate seam allowance. These are available as a magnetic guide that sticks to the throat plate or in a T-shaped screw-on form. Once I had the School of Sewing students try one, they were hooked.

PINS

Don't underestimate the importance of pinning. I use a variety of pins: glass head pins won't be melted by your iron, flower head pins are easy to grab, curved safety pins are used for basting quilts, and fork pins are useful when sewing patchwork seams. Thicker pins are used for thicker fabrics. Your pincushion might come with pins, but I promise you a set of glass head pins or flower head pins will serve you far better.

PINCUSHION

My favorite is a magnetic version. I can sew along, pulling out pins and tossing them at my pincushion. Passing it over my sewing table or the floor makes for easy clean up, too. Bonus points if it comes with a cover, which makes it great to take to class.

HAND-SEWING NEEDLES

These typically come in a circular package containing a variety of sizes, each meant for a different type of fabric or project: bigger needles for tough, thick fabrics and smaller needles for thin and delicate work.

▶ *See Glossary for: needle threader and thimble.*

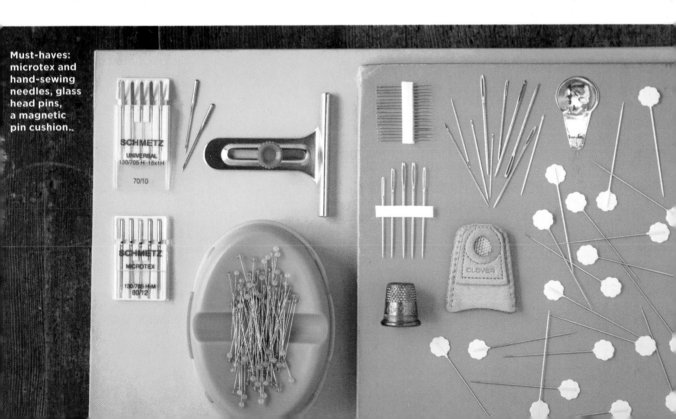

Must-haves: microtex and hand-sewing needles, glass head pins, a magnetic pin cushion..

Pressing Supplies

IRON

A good iron that can be used with steam or no steam is a must. No need to blow the budget here — just look for something heavy. A sharp point is nice for pressing in tight areas.

IRONING BOARD OR PRESSING BOARD

Most ironing boards aren't firm enough to get very flat seams. If you think a lot of sewing is in your future, you might like a pressing board, which can be made any size. Check out the frequently updated page of tutorial references at our theschoolofsewing.com website for a pressing board tutorial link.

SPRAY STARCH

Steam and pressing are fine, but using a starch (page 63) makes seams lay perfectly flat and stay that way. I especially recommend using this on fabric that is cut on the bias to minimize stretching. A variety of options exist, but my favorite is Mary Ellen's Best Press, a starch alternative. I use so much of this that I buy it by the gallon.

"It amazed me how much of a difference spray starch made for making our quilt tops! Those blocks stayed flat and went together perfectly." —AMY

SEAM ROLL AND PRESSING HAM

Pressing a flat quilt block is one thing. Pressing a 3-D object, like a shirt sleeve or a purse corner, is another. Seam rolls and pressing hams are stuffed into your project, allowing the iron to press only the seam or area in question without leaving behind unwanted creases in other areas. A rolled towel is a decent seam roll substitute.

TURNING TOOLS

Any time you need to turn a sewing project right side out, you'll want to get the corners poked out nicely. A point turner or chopstick comes in handy for this job. Similarly, a bodkin is used for turning a tube right side out. A common safety pin is an excellent bodkin.

▶ *See Glossary for: hem guide, bias tape maker, pressing cloth, and sleeve board.*

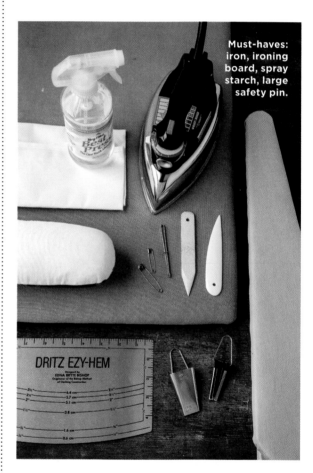

Must-haves: iron, ironing board, spray starch, large safety pin.

DRITZ EZY-HEM

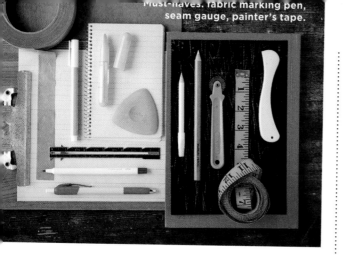

SEAM GAUGE

These inexpensive tools with a sliding marker are excellent for measuring and marking seam allowances and hems.

FABRIC MARKING PENS AND PENCILS

Use these to mark seams, cutting lines, guidelines, and button placements on your project. Some pens erase with a mist of water or are air erase pens, with marks disappearing in a short time. Others, such as the Pilot FriXion pen, erase with friction or heat. White chalk pencils are especially great for marking on dark fabrics. I recommend having at least two different types in your set of supplies, one for working on light fabrics and another on darker fabrics.

▶ *See Glossary for: chaco liner, tailor's chalk, tracing wheel, measuring tape, and Hera marker.*

Marking Supplies

PAINTER'S TAPE

So many uses! Easily mark a straight line for machine quilting, number quilt blocks to stay organized, or mark specific measurements on acrylic rulers.

TYPES OF THREAD

When it comes to thread, the different types can be overwhelming to a beginner. Here's a quick primer.

1. **ALL-PURPOSE:** Used for projects in this book and for the majority of the sewing you'll likely do.

2. **VARIEGATED:** Adds a unique finish to topstitching, decorative stitches, or quilting.

3. **EMBROIDERY:** Use all or some of the six strands in this floss to add hand-embroidered touches to your project.

4. **INVISIBLE:** A great choice for zigzagging around the edges of appliqué.

5. **METALLIC:** Add a sparkly finish to your project with this thread.

6. **VINTAGE:** Beautiful to look at or to display in mason jars, but don't use it for actual sewing as old threads dry out and break easily.

The thickness of threads vary: thinner for finer fabrics, thicker for fabrics like denim. Choose the best quality you can afford as it lasts longer, sews stronger seams, and is less likely to break. When matching threads to fabrics, a slightly darker thread than your fabric will blend better than a lighter one. My thread stash is full of Aurifil 50wt and Gutermann spools. Start with neutrals such as white, cream, gray, and black, then gradually add smaller spools of specific colors to coordinate with fabrics for your projects.

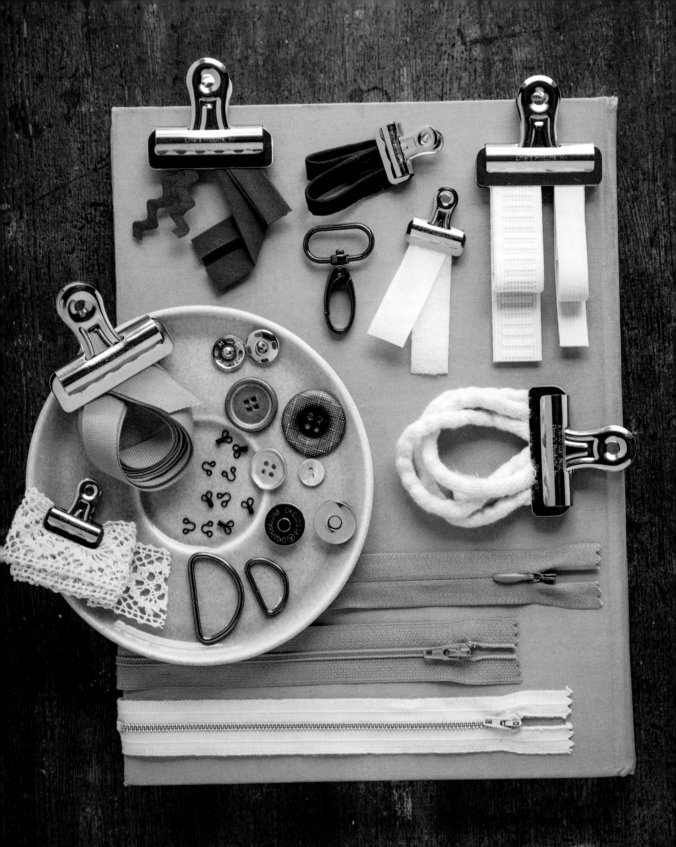

Must-haves: zippers,
hook and loop tape,
magnetic snaps,
buttons, D-rings.

Know Your Notions

ZIPPERS

We'll use all-purpose zippers in our beginner projects, but invisible zippers are available, too. Zippers can be separating, as used in a jacket, or non-separating and closed at one end, like pants zippers. Look for long pull zippers, which are easy to grab and pull open.

HOOK AND LOOP TAPE

Commonly referred to as Velcro, hook and loop tape comes in several widths and both sew-in and adhesive varieties.

BUTTONS

Buttons are used on projects in both decorative and functional ways. The choices can be mind-boggling at times! Pay close attention to the specific size called for in a pattern.

MAGNETIC SNAPS

These give your bag or purse project a professional look without taking a lot of time to install.

D-RINGS AND SWIVEL CLASPS

D-rings come in a variety of widths and are often used in bags, belts, or, in our case, the Ruffled Wristlet Key Fob. Swivel clasps come in handy for the Carry-All Clutch.

▶ *See Glossary for: bias tape, piping, snaps, hook and eye, ribbon, rickrack, and elastic.*

Other Supplies

A few goodies to round out your School of Sewing supply list. These aren't essential, but can help make your sewing experience a little easier, especially if you are moving sewing areas frequently back and forth to class.

BOBBIN BOX

If you often change thread colors, having threaded extra bobbins on hand is a smart idea. Keep them in order in a small bobbin box for easy organization.

TOOLBOX

Having a container to hold and transport supplies is extremely helpful. Plus, your supplies are easily corralled in your workspace. While you can always get an official sewing box, a tool or tackle box from the hardware store or a cosmetics organizer also make great choices.

"My bobbin box is so fantastic! No more half unwound bobbins floating around in the bottom of my sewing bag!" —CALI

SEWING MACHINE CASE OR TOTE

Especially useful if you will be traveling to and from a sewing class, a case or tote can make carting your machine easier and will also protect your machine. Look for a case or tote that has room for your extra presser feet, cords, and maybe even your basic sewing supplies. Some cases have handles and wheels like rolling luggage.

BRIGHT LIGHT

Even the brightest machine light may not illuminate your workspace, especially if you sew at nighttime. A bendable desk lamp can work well, but lights specific to sewing or handwork are great options as they have bulbs that closely mimic daylight, and some can even be mounted to your sewing machine.

A FABRIC STORE
FIELD TRIP

Fabric Stores Galore

▸ Feeding Your Stash

INDEPENDENT FABRIC SHOPS

Typically, these local fabric stores carry quilting cottons and home decor fabrics, notions, and a wide variety of sewing patterns. Some shops carry a certain style of fabric (such as vintage reproduction or bold modern prints), while others carry a little of everything. Independent shops are very likely to have employees who sew, can answer specific questions, and can make recommendations about products, patterns, or fabric types. Some brick and mortar shops also have an online store component.

ONLINE RETAILERS

If your local shops don't carry the types of fabrics you are looking for, online stores are a great option. You can't feel the fabrics, of course, and computer screens don't always reflect the exact color of a fabric, so don't be afraid to call or e-mail to ask for help coordinating your order. Check the descriptions for the exact scale of a print so you aren't surprised when your order arrives. Sets of swatches, called "color cards," for some solid fabric lines are nice to have and are available from several manufacturers. One of my favorite online shops, Pink Chalk Fabrics, has talked me through color options over the phone and has mailed swatches to help with decision making.

CHAIN STORES

For finding things like interfacings, batting, and notions, chain stores are a great option if you don't have an independent shop nearby. They carry a variety of fabrics from quilting cottons to garment fabrics, as well as commercial brand garment sewing patterns. Fabric prices can be lower than at independent shops, but keep in mind that the fabric itself may not be as high quality. Feel for yourself to check the difference (see Hand in the Glossary). You're less likely to find employees who

sew and are able to answer your project-specific questions at chain stores. Additionally, because most manufacturers of designer fabrics sell their fabrics only to independent brick and mortar or online shops, you won't be able to find many collections of coordinating designer prints.

Fabric-ology

SELECTING FABRICS

Shopping for fabric is incredibly fun. The options seem limitless! As a general rule, I look for quilting cotton prints and solids that can be used in everything from clothes and bags to quilts and curtains. Stick to fabrics from the Easier-to-Sew list (see below) and look for fabrics that are washable. Avoid dry clean only fabrics, especially if your project will get a lot of use. If possible jot down or snap a photo of the information printed on the bolt end, in order to have the fabric design name in case you need to purchase more. Always ask yourself two questions when choosing fabric for your project:

1. Do I like the way the fabric looks?

2. Does the type of fabric suit my project?

Never let #1 override #2. No matter how amazing a certain print is, if it's the wrong type of fabric to use, your project will not be enjoyable to sew.

In general, I recommend using woven fabrics over knits or stretchy fabrics. In woven fabrics, threads run horizontally and vertically to form the fabric. Knits are made with loops of thread, which allows the fabric to stretch.

EASIER-TO-SEW FABRICS

These are the fabrics we used in our School of Sewing, as they are a little easier for a beginner to use. Selection can be overwhelming, so I recommend sticking with these types of fabric for projects in this book.

Quilting Cotton

We used these fabrics for 90% of our School of Sewing projects. Prints, solids, and near solids — so many amazing options are on the market! They are truly versatile and adding a variety of interfacings

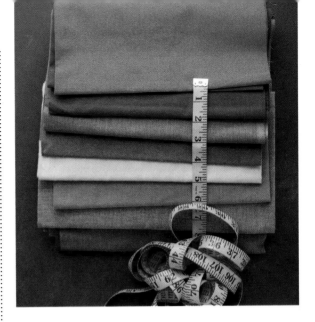

can make these fabrics act like thicker home decor fabrics or even like water resistant laminate fabric.

Home Decor

Great for bags, upholstery, or any other project where you want a sturdy and stiffer feel to the fabric. Not all home decor fabrics are created equal —some can be machine washed, but not all, so be sure to check the bolt end for care info.

Voile

This stuff is luxurious! You have to feel it to understand just how wonderfully it drapes (see Drape in the Glossary). It's usually 54" wide and can be slippery to sew, so be sure to use fine pins. Voile is a good choice for the Speedy Pillowcase project for an extra smooth place to rest your head.

Laminate Fabrics

These are cotton fabrics coated on one side in a thin, clear polyurethane laminate (PUL) film. Water-resistant laminate can be used to make bibs, raincoats, and bags, among other things. Use Wonder Clips or paper clips instead of pins, which will leave permanent holes in this fabric.

Muslin

Very inexpensive and often used for trying out a new design first without using a precious printed fabric, or for testing the fit of a garment pattern. Consider using muslin to try out things like decorative stitches or free motion quilting.

Shirting

This can be brand-new from the bolt or repurposed from shirts found at thrift stores or a closet in your house. Using dress shirts can create a sentimental gift. Watch the grainline when cutting, since it is not yardage from a bolt. Cut apart shirts at the seams to maximize the sizes of each piece.

Wool Felt

Much thicker and more luxurious than its inexpensive acrylic craft felt relative, wool felt is often used in home decor projects or for creating stuffed animals (often called softies). An added bonus? Its raw edges won't fray.

Flannel

Cozy and soft, flannel makes a great choice for the Speedy Pillowcase project. Be sure to clean lint from your machine often when using this type of fabric.

Canvas

Similar to cotton duck and utility fabric, canvas is very durable. It's good for tote bags or for adding stiffness between layers in a zipper pouch. Because of its thickness, use a denim needle.

NOT-SO-EASY FABRICS

While they are wonderful in their own right, the following fabrics are not recommended for School of Sewing projects in this book. These finicky fabrics can be troublesome for a beginner and may require special needles and presser feet.

• Satin • Corduroy • Knit • Tulle • Vinyl • Denim • Suede • Felt • Silk • Fleece • Wool • Linen
(An exception would be a cotton/linen blend such as Essex Linen from Robert Kaufman Fabrics. These are fantastic!)

TYPES OF PRINTS
Directional vs. Non-Directional

Non-directional prints look the same no matter which way you turn them, making them very forgiving in any project. Directional prints can be one-way, which means that the fabric looks correct in only one direction, or two-way, as in a stripe or chevron.

Large-Scale vs. Small-Scale

Small-scale prints hide seams more easily and can be more approachable for a beginner in cutting, too. Large-scale prints are best for projects that have sizable pieces, like tote bags or quilt backings. Cutting large-scale prints into small pieces reduces the impact of the design. Watch out for large-scale stripes and chevrons, as beginners may find it difficult to make the design stay straight along the seam when cutting.

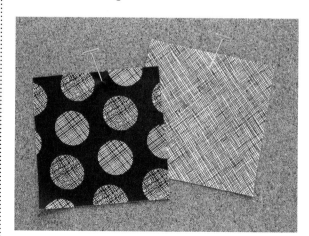

TYPES OF SOLIDS

Solids

Solids are easy for beginners to work with because the fabric is virtually identical on both sides. This eliminates the worry over which is the right side. Additionally, solids are often less expensive than prints, making them a cost-effective choice.

Near-Solids

Near-solids have a slight texture to them when viewed closely but read as a solid from a distance. Some near-solids, such as shot cottons and cross-woven fabrics, are made of two different thread colors—one for the warp and one for the weft. The thread colors combine to give a beautiful dimension to the fabric. I include linen/cotton blends into this category as well.

"I learned that the quality of home decor fabric can vary. The kind I purchased, while super cute, was too slippery and not easy to sew with when I made my apron."
—CALI

FABRIC VOCABULARY

Right Side vs. Wrong Side

Easier to spot on a printed fabric, the right side contains the print and is what will show on the outside of a finished project.

Selvage

Running along the edge of the yardage, the selvage often has fabric information (manufacturer, designer, fabric collection name) and provides a more densely woven finished edge that prevents raveling. Solids do not have a printed selvage.

Bias

Running at a 45-degree angle from the selvage edge, the bias is stretchy. Try pulling on fabric along this line to see how it behaves differently than pulling along the grainline (page 46). Notice how much more flexible it is? This feature makes it excellent for sewing pieces that need to flex around a curve. But watch out — the bias should always be handled carefully as the fabric can easily stretch out of shape.

PRE-CUTS

Sold by several fabric manufacturers, pre-cuts are just that: yardage, often from a single fabric collection (page 49), that has been cut to a specific size. They are great time-savers, but you will pay a bit more per yard.

Fat Quarters

A fat quarter and a ¼ yard cut from a bolt have the same area, but because of the way a fat quarter is cut, it offers more usable cutting area (see below). They are sold in pre-cut bundles or individually and are a great way to collect smaller cuts from a variety of fabrics.

▶ *See Glossary for: fat eighths, jelly roll strips, layer cakes, and charm squares.*

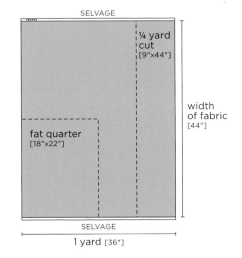

Grainline

Also referred to as the warp threads, these threads run along the length of the fabric, parallel to the selvage. When you see an arrow on a printed pattern template, it should always be placed along the grainline.

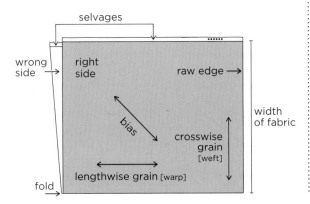

Crossgrain

Also referred to as the weft threads, these threads run from selvage to selvage across the width of the fabric.

Raw Edge

The exposed threads left on a cut end of a piece of fabric. Left unfinished, the threads will begin to fray.

Width of Fabric

The distance from selvage to selvage. Quilting cotton comes on bolts of fabric about 44" wide. That width includes the selvage, so assume a 40" to 42" width of usable fabric. Many apparel and home decor fabrics are 60" wide and come on bolts or rolled on tubes.

▶ *See Glossary for: drape and hand.*

Color Theory Crash Course

▶ Choosing the Perfect Colors

For many, School of Sewing students included, picking fabrics is wildly fun...except for the pesky part about selecting color combinations. Keep these color theory basics in mind for your next project. Consider them a buffet of options, rather than a set of rules that must all be followed.

▶ **TIP**

When in doubt, always go with one fabric that you truly love, then add other fabrics by picking out colors from your main print.

"To pick the fabrics for my quilt, I found a beautiful image of a bedroom in a home decor magazine. The colors used became my fabric shopping list!" —CHRISTINE

AROUND THE COLOR WHEEL

Such a beautiful thing, the rainbow of a color wheel. You're familiar with the primary colors — red, yellow, and blue — and their secondary friends — orange, green, and violet — but there's so much more the wheel can teach us about the relationship among colors. That blue-green you love so much? It's a tertiary color, formed by mixing a primary and secondary color together. Colors work together in some pretty amazing ways. Consider the following color harmonies.

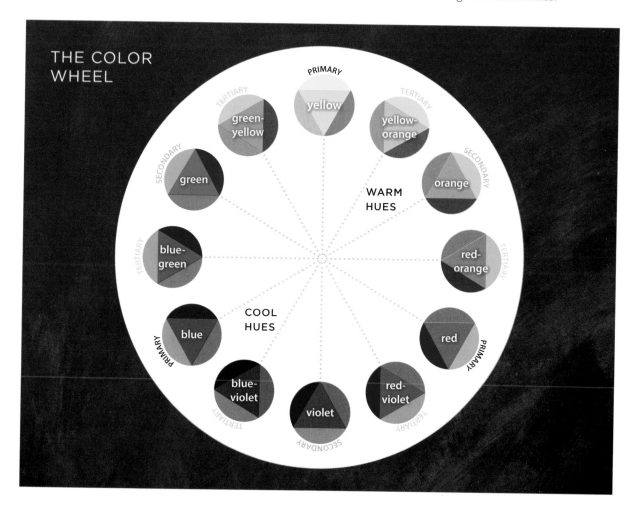

THE COLOR WHEEL

PRIMARY — yellow
TERTIARY — green-yellow
TERTIARY — yellow-orange
SECONDARY — green
SECONDARY — orange
WARM HUES
TERTIARY — blue-green
TERTIARY — red-orange
PRIMARY — red
COOL HUES
PRIMARY — blue
TERTIARY — blue-violet
SECONDARY — violet
TERTIARY — red-violet

ANALOGOUS

COMPLEMENTARY

MONOCHROMATIC

SPLIT COMPLEMENT

Monochromatic Colors

Light to dark versions of one color.

Analogous Colors

Colors that appear side by side on the color wheel, making them calm and pleasing to the eye. Make sure there is enough contrast between them to avoid a muddled look.

Complementary Colors

Colors that are opposite each other on the color wheel, creating a lot of contrast. These combinations should be used carefully as this introduces a lot of movement that can be jarring.

Split Complement

This variation of complementary uses the adjacent colors for one-half of the complement.

Triad

Three colors spread evenly around the color wheel. In combination, they are quite vibrant, so try to use one as the dominant color with the remaining two in smaller roles. Or, try picking and using only two of the three colors in the triad.

TRIAD

Warm vs. Cool

Do you want your project to have a decidedly warm or cool feel? If so, direct your fabric hunting in that direction. Warms are reds, oranges, and yellows. For cool colors, think blue, green, and violet.

Neutrals

Using solids and neutrals can calm a design. These include white, gray, and black, of course, but also creams, tans, and browns. Cotton linen blends are excellent neutrals, as the subtle differences in thread color can tame adjacent prints. Consider making a project entirely out of neutrals in varying degrees of light and dark.

SPRING BOARDS OF INSPIRATION

▸ Inspiration for your color choices can come from anywhere. For example, when you are drawn to a photograph or an image, ask yourself what colors you are most attracted to.

▸ Keep an inspiration board or notebook with clippings, paint chips, photos, and fabric swatches that excite you.

▸ Consult the selvage edge of a printed fabric. The colored dots represent the colors used in the print. Use these to coordinate solids with your fabric.

▸ Look at packaging and advertisements in the grocery or bookstore. Try to pick out what color harmony the designer used.

PRE-WASHING: THE GREAT DEBATE

Pre-washing means washing and drying a fabric before sewing in order to allow for any shrinking or bleeding of dye to happen before the fabric is sewn. It is an often debated topic among sewists and quilters. Luckily, quilt-shop quality fabrics of today do not often bleed. When making a garment, pre-washing is a must so that all shrinkage occurs prior to sewing. For quilts, pre-washing is not necessary as long as you are using quilt-shop quality fabrics. Skipping the pre-washing step and saving the washing and drying for after the quilt is finished results in a cozy crinkly quilt, perfect for cuddling.

If mixing new yardage with vintage or repurposed fabrics, pre-wash everything.

If you do pre-wash, consider these tips:

▸ Use a Color Catcher in the wash to prevent light or white fabrics from picking up colored dye.

▸ Prevent raveling by snipping corners or trimming edges with pinking shears.

▸ After washing and drying, thoroughly iron your fabric (straight from the dryer is easiest) to prepare it for accurate cutting.

WHAT'S A FABRIC COLLECTION?

Designer fabrics often come in collections. These are sets of designs, made in complementary color palates, typically with a nice mix of large and small-scale prints, stripes, and all-over designs. Fabric companies may also recommend solid fabrics that coordinate with specific lines.

Interfacing 101

▸ **What's the Difference?**

Interfacing is an amazing thing! It adds weight, body, and thickness to fabrics and is what makes a tote bag stand up to hold your gear instead of falling to the floor in a fabric puddle. However, staring down the wall-o-interfacings can be pretty intimidating to the beginner, because those interfacing bolts look alike! Keep in mind that you won't be using everything you see in the store. For our projects, I focused on only a handful of interfacing products to help get you more familiar with each one. Here are some things to consider.

FUSIBLE VS. SEW-IN

Fusible is easier for beginners. Use the heat of your iron, often in combination with a damp press cloth or mist of water from a spray bottle, to fuse the interfacing to the wrong side of your fabric. The fusible side can be identified by its tiny bumpy glue dots or its shiny surface. Use muslin or a pressing cloth above and below your project to prevent glue from sticking to your iron or ironing board. If this happens, use a dryer sheet to remove sticky substance from your iron. Sew-in interfacing is slightly less stiff than fusible interfacing. It is basted to the wrong side of the fabric by sewing outside the regular seam allowance, so that the basting stitches do not show in the final project.

▸ **TIP**

Rather than cutting out the fabric and the interfacing and then fusing them together, whenever possible fuse the interfacing to the fabric and then cut out the shape to save time. Use this technique for the Tech Case flap and for the Carry-All Clutch.

WOVEN VS. NON-WOVEN

Woven interfacing allows the drape of fabric to remain. Non-woven makes fabrics more stiff but sacrifices the drape.

I sometimes use two layers of woven interfacing to make a quilting cotton feel more like a home decor fabric, as done in the Pleated Purse project. Try it for yourself!

THICKNESS AND WEIGHT

Confusion over which weight to purchase is common, so it is important to know your intended purpose. Do you want a stiff and sturdy bag or do you prefer a more floppy and crushable bag? Debating between featherweight or heavyweight? Most often, aim to match interfacing weight to the thickness of the fabric. When in doubt, try a small sample of each on the wrong side of a scrap from your project. Usually these mock-ups will allow a clear winner to appear.

Two of my favorite Pellon products are its Fusible Fleece and fusible Thermolam. Both give some padding to your project, with Thermolam being just slightly thicker, adding some extra heft. This makes it an excellent choice for projects like the Essential Tote Bag. I have used both to make everything from place mats and sewing machine covers to bags and Christmas stockings.

GENERAL TIPS

▸ Pay attention to widths on the bolt. Interfacings range from 20" to 45" wide. Some come prepackaged in 1 yard cuts.

▸ Always read the manufacturer instructions that are included in the paper wrapped on the bolt with the interfacing.

▸ Pay close attention to information on bolt ends and ask for help when in doubt about which product is right for your project.

RELATED PRODUCTS

Paper-Backed Fusible Web

Sold under the names WonderUnder and HeatnBond, this magical product is perfect for adding appliqué to your project (see Appliqué 101, page 101).

Quilt Batting

An entire chapter could be devoted to the different types of batting on the market, but I'll cut to the chase and recommend an all-cotton

"I accidentally bought non-fusible fleece once and could not, for the life of me, understand what I was doing wrong when I was 'ironing' it to the fabric." —PAM

or cotton/polyester blend of low-loft (thinner) batting. It is sold by the yard from giant bolts or in prepackaged cuts based on standard bed sizes. Other options include polyester, bamboo, wool, or silk battings, and each quilter has a different favorite. Each type varies in thickness, weight, warmth, and how much they shrink when washed. Pay close attention to how far apart your machine quilting can be spaced, too, as each batting is different. You don't want your project to become lumpy over time due to batting that moves about. Experiment to see what you prefer and you'll soon find a favorite go-to product.

▸ *See Glossary for: interlining, heat-resistant batting, and fusible hem tape.*

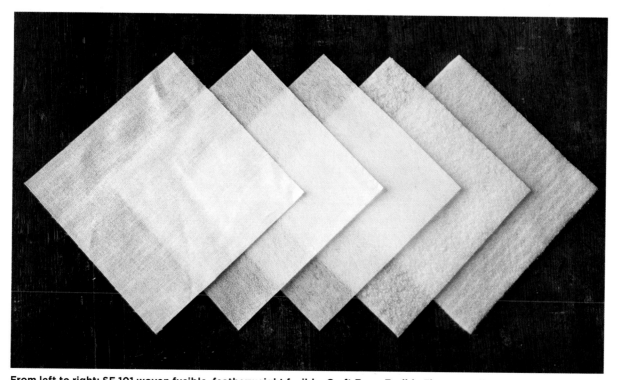

From left to right: SF 101 woven fusible, featherweight fusible, Craft Fuse, Fusible Fleece, Fusible Thermolam.

DRIVER'S ED
BASIC SKILLS AND GENERAL TIPS

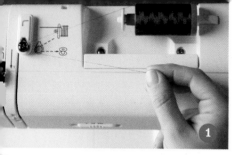

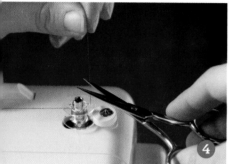

IMPROPERLY
WOUND
BOBBIN

PROPE
WOL
BOB

Wind 'Er Up!

▶ How to Wind and Load a Bobbin

Bobbin troubles can be a stumbling block for many beginners. Most thread tension issues stem from an improperly wound or loaded bobbin. But it doesn't have to be that way. Grab your sewing machine's manual and this section to work step by step through the process; it is slightly different for each manufacturer. It's also important to know that not all bobbins are created equally. Some are metal and others are clear plastic. Bobbins are specific to each machine, and even clear plastic bobbins have differences, so buy exactly what your machine manual says. Take it from Whitney, who can wind and load bobbins like a pro now — you can do this!

"I used my sewing machine in college to make a few projects. Then the bobbin ran out. I got frustrated and couldn't figure out how to wind the bobbin right, so I stuck my machine in a closet. For years!" —WHITNEY

WINDING THE BOBBIN

1. Insert the thread spool onto the spool pin, using a disc to hold the spool in place. Pull the loose end of the thread under the thread guide and to the bobbin winder tension disc. Wrap the thread around the bobbin winder, going in the direction described in your manual. Be sure the thread is actually in the tension disc.

2. Insert the thread into the hole of a completely empty bobbin. The thread should enter from the inside and exit on the outside.

3. Snap the bobbin onto the bobbin winder and push to the right until it clicks into place. For some machines, you may need to push the stop toward the bobbin instead.

4. While holding the thread tail, push the foot pedal to begin winding the bobbin. After a few spins, lift your foot from the foot pedal to stop the winding. Clip the loose thread tail close to the bobbin. Press the foot pedal and continue winding.

   Note: If the presser foot goes up and down when winding the bobbin, stop pressing and pull out on the handwheel to disengage the clutch. Continue winding the bobbin. Remember to push the handwheel in when the bobbin is full. Most mechanical machines operate this way.

5. When full, the bobbin should automatically stop. Push the bobbin pin to the left and clip the thread, leaving a few inches of thread tail.

INSERTING THE BOBBIN
Top-Loading/Drop-in Bobbin

You'll know you have a top-loading/drop-in bobbin if there is a see-through cover just under your presser foot. Celebrate if you do, because this style means fewer steps and the added bonus of being able to see when the bobbin is low on thread.

Refer to your machine's manual and pay close attention to the direction the thread comes off the bobbin. That actually matters! Most often, the thread will come off the bobbin on the left side, and will make the letter P.

1. Drop the bobbin into the case inside the machine, holding on to the thread tail.

2. Pull the thread tail into the slit in the bobbin case and pull it along the path as indicated in your manual.

3. Replace the clear cover over the case. We'll take care of that thread tail when we thread the upper part of the machine.

Front-Loading Bobbin

If you have a front-loading bobbin, have no fear. There are a few more specifics to grasp, but once you get the hang of it, you will be just fine. The first thing to understand is that the bobbin case is the only thing to remove from your machine! Don't be tempted to remove the entire bobbin mechanism (I have seen this done!).

1. Look for a latch to pull open that will release the bobbin case from the machine.

2. Insert the bobbin with the thread coming off in the direction indicated in your manual. Pull the thread tail through the slot in the case, then bring it around to the thread guide on the case.

3. Hold the case by the latch as you insert it into the machine and release the latch. You'll know it is in correctly when you hear a small click. You may need to push and wiggle it slightly to find the right spot.

GENERAL TIPS

▶ Always match the top and bottom/bobbin thread brand and usually the color, too.

▶ Never add thread to a bobbin that is not empty.

▶ If your machine is not marked with the correct thread direction for loading your bobbin, use painter's tape and a marker to do it yourself. Eventually, you'll know that direction by heart.

▶ Watch out for improperly wound bobbins. The threads should wind even and tight, not sponge-like and top/bottom heavy.

▶ I like to have several wound bobbins on hand in case I need to change thread colors quickly or if I am quilting and want to avoid stopping to refill a bobbin.

TOP-LOADING/DROP-IN BOBBIN

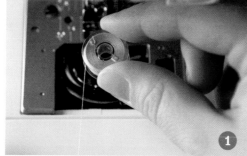

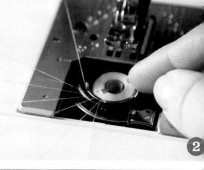

FRONT-LOADING BOBBIN

Threading a Sewing Machine

Rule #1: Don't be overwhelmed. Or at least try not to be. Like the bobbin winding paths, the paths for threading machines vary by machine manufacturer, so keep your manual handy. It is extremely important that you get your thread through *all* the thread guides specific to your machine. One skipped step will result in unbalanced and uneven stitches. Now, let's do this!

THE TOP THREAD

Be sure your presser foot is up. Believe it or not, this ensures a smooth path through the guides and tension discs. Also ensure that the needle is fully inserted and the needle screw is tight. Place the thread spool securely on the spool pin. Pay attention to the direction the thread should come off the spool; your manual should tell you. Most newer machines have numbered guides imprinted on the machine to help you with threading.

1. Pull the thread off the spool and through the first thread guide on the top of your machine. Skip the bobbin winder tension discs for this step!

2. Pull the tail forward toward you and down to the bottom of the narrow slot, around the U-turn curve, then back up to the take-up lever.

3. Guide the thread into the take-up lever by either sliding it in the slot or pushing it through a hole. The take-up lever should be in the highest position, so you may need to turn the handwheel a bit here.

4. Once through the take-up lever, bring the thread tail back down the previous slot to the needle guides. There are usually two thread guides here. Look for the first one on the lower front of the machine. The last thread guide is actually just above the needle. Slide the thread behind this needle bar. Many people miss this step, so look carefully! Once it is through this thread guide, the thread should come straight down, almost parallel to the needle.

5. Now you can thread the needle. Always thread the needle from front to back. If you have trouble seeing the eye and you don't have a needle threader handy, try guiding the very tip of the thread along the length of the needle. Every needle has a groove, leading straight to the eye. Follow it and you should be through that eye easily. Use a freshly cut thread tail and moisten it if needed.

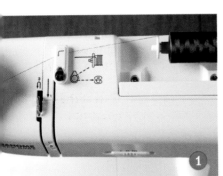

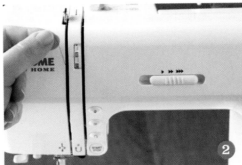

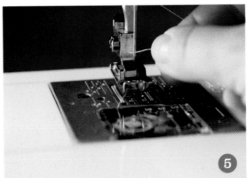

BRINGING UP THE BOBBIN THREAD

▶ AUTOMATIC NEEDLE THREADERS

Many newer machines have a built-in needle threader, which makes for handy and quick needle threading. Refer to your manual and use this feature if you have one. It is definitely worth taking a few minutes to learn!

Essentially, you'll raise the needle to its highest position and pull down the needle threader, which inserts a hook into the eye of the needle. Each model varies after this step, but as you guide the thread into the thread guides and release the needle threader, the hook pulls a loop of your thread through the eye of the needle, and you're ready to sew!

BRINGING UP THE BOBBIN THREAD

Holding on to the upper thread tail, turn the handwheel toward you to move the needle up and down once. This brings the bobbin thread up. Move both thread tails to the back of the presser foot by sweeping under the presser foot, using the tip of your scissors or seam ripper or (my favorite trick) hold the top thread with two hands and sweep it under the presser foot.

If you have a needle up/down button, press it twice while holding the upper thread tail. The bobbin thread pops up easily!

Yay, you! You did it! If you've been holding your breath, you can relax now! Now that you're a machine threading pro, take it out and do it all over again. Nope. I'm not kidding! Practice makes perfect, right?

"Do yourself a favor and get a machine with an automatic needle threader. You can thank me later!" —CALI

Favorite Tips

Below are a few basics to get you on your way. Refer to these tips often. Before you know it, they will become second nature.

HANDS ARE FOR STEERING

Don't push or pull the fabric. Simply steer the fabric and let the feed dogs do the work. Lightly lay your hands on either side of your project and guide as needed, keeping your eye on the seam allowance. Practice sewing along the lines on lined notebook paper.

PIN EARLY AND PIN OFTEN

My mom's favorite phrase was "When in doubt, pin it to death." Pinning makes a big difference for such a small investment of time, especially around curves or at seams that need to match. Match raw edges together and pin perpendicular to the edge of the fabric, weaving the pin into and out of fabric to grip in two places.

Always remove pins as they near the presser foot. A magnetic pin cushion is a perfect place to corral those removed pins! Whatever you do, never sew over pins.

I recommend pinning at each end, then at the center, and continuing to pin at midpoints until there are pins every 2" to 3".

SEAM ALLOWANCES MATTER

The seam allowance is the distance from the raw edge of the fabric to the stitching line or needle. If sewn with the wrong size seam allowance, your project will be either too large or too small. Projects in this book call for a ½" or ¼" seam allowance. Look closely at the foot plate on your machine and you'll notice groves with marked seam allowances showing the distance to the center needle position. These are handy but can be hard to see. When accuracy counts (and that's often!) use a seam guide.

Measure the distance from the edge of your all-purpose presser foot to the center needle position by placing a measuring tape, acrylic ruler, or seam gauge under your presser foot and slowly lowering the needle to touch it. You may be able to adjust your needle position so that lining up your fabric with the edge of the presser foot yields a ¼″ seam.

USE A SEAM GUIDE

If you want an accurate and consistent seam allowance, a seam guide will be your best friend. My favorite type is the screw-in cloth guide variety. I use it daily! A magnetic seam guide works in the same way and is not specific to one brand of machine. A stack of Post-it notes stuck to the machine bed does the trick, too! When it loses its grip, simply pull off the bottom sheet. In a pinch, use repositionable painter's tape or even slip a rubber band over the throat plate.

SEW WITH A FABRIC LEADER SCRAP

If your fabric won't feed through the needle or, worse, gets pulled down into the needle hole when you begin to stitch, I highly recommend using a leader (often referred to as an anchor cloth). Simply grab a scrap of fabric, fold it on to itself, and stick it under your needle. Sew the leader and, without snipping threads, butt your project up against the scrap to continue sewing. The stitching in the cloth will guide your project under the presser foot much more easily. Your scrap can be used over and over again.

NEEDLE POSITIONS

Many machines allow you to move the needle to the left or right. Never underestimate this. It's incredibly useful for sewing zippers and topstitching and edgestitching. Just be careful! If you're changing presser feet often for a specific project, you'll want to check to be sure your needle will clear the opening in each presser foot. No one likes a broken needle!

Stitch-ology

▶ Types of Stitches and When to Use Them

A straight stitch may be what comes to mind when you hear the word "sewing" but there is so much more! Some stitches are functional and have a special purpose, while others are purely decorative. Refer to your manual for the specific stitches on your machine, because in some cases you may need to switch presser feet. Play around with your machine and get to know each other. Try out all the stitches possible on your machine, and your first project will be much more successful. What are you waiting for? Grab some fabric and get sewing! Stitches shown left to right on page 52-53.

STRAIGHT STITCH

The most valuable player on the stitch team. A straight stitch will be used most of the time you sew and can be sewn with or without a backstitch (see below).

ZIGZAG

Zigzag stitches are useful for keeping raw edges of fabric from raveling. Your zigzag can take on a variety of widths and lengths by changing the settings (see Adjusting Stitches, page 59). You can even sew back and forth in one spot by setting the stitch length to 0. This is especially handy if your machine can sew on a button with a button foot.

BACKSTITCH

To keep your stitches from coming loose at the ends of the fabric, you'll want to sew a backstitch, which simply means sewing forward, then backward a few stitches, then forward again. Your machine will have either a lever or a button to press to make your machine sew backward, and it will be marked with an icon that looks like a curved arrow. Sew a seam with and without a backstitch. Now try to pull them apart. See the difference? Always use a backstitch when the seam will receive a lot of wear and tear.

LOCKSTITCH

Engage this feature and your machine will sew in one place for a few stitches, creating a knot and securing your stitch just as a backstitch does.

BASTING STITCH

Machine basting is useful for holding fabrics together temporarily (such as pleats) before sewing a final seam. Increase your stitch length to the highest number to make the stitches easier to remove. Machine basting is not the same as basting a quilt, which is outlined on page 39.

STRETCH/KNIT STITCH

Sewing a regular straight stitch won't work with knit fabrics. To allow the fabric to move and stretch after sewing, you'll use a stretch stitch.

DECORATIVE STITCH

These are available on electronic and computerized sewing machines and look like everything from letters and blanket stitches to star shapes and even tiny cats. Adjusting the stitch length and width changes the look of these stitches, too.

TOPSTITCH

One way to really add a professional finish to any project is to add topstitching. Look at the clothes you are wearing or a favorite bag you own. If you see any stitches on top of the fabric and close to a seam, that's topstitching, and it is done at a variety of seam allowances. These stitches will show, so pay close attention to thread color, use a topstitch needle if possible, and take your time.

EDGESTITCH

An edgestitch (page 82) is often done at ⅛" or ¹⁄₁₆" away from a seam.

ADJUSTING STITCHES
Stitch Length

The stitch length might be adjusted by turning a knob or pressing a button. It's important to understand that the shorter the stitch, the stronger the seam. In general, longer stitches have a looser hold, and, while easier to seam rip, they also mean a more weak seam. Longer stitches are used for basting something in place or gathering a ruffle. If you want zigzags closer together, as in a satin stitch, use a smaller length. Shorter stitch lengths are good for sewing curves. The stitch length I most often use is 2.0mm stitch length.

Stitch Width

Also adjusted by turning a knob or pressing a button, stitch width sets the side to side distance for zigzag and decorative stitches.

MAKE A STITCH CHEAT SHEET

Making a stitch sampler takes the guess work out of remembering stitch settings and also allows you to get a feel for all that your machine can do. Grab two layers of fabric and stitch a variety of seams, and use a pen to note the specific length and width that you used for each stitch. Keep this cheat sheet handy for reference during future projects.

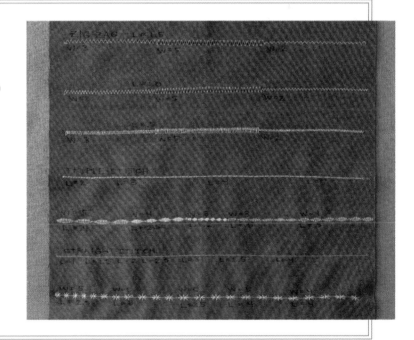

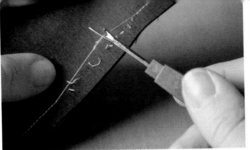

Seam Ripping 101

Un-sewing is just as vital to the success of your project as sewing. Even the best sewists make mistakes and understand that a seam ripper is your friend and not the enemy. In other words, don't fear the seam ripper!

HOW TO USE A SEAM RIPPER

Insert the sharp point of the seam ripper into the middle of a stitch on one side of your project. Slide the seam ripper in until the thread is clipped. Then move down three or four stitches and repeat, continuing in this manner the whole length of the seam you wish to rip. Then turn the seam over and gently pull the thread from the reverse side, which should pull away easily. Snip this thread, then brush away the stitches ripped on the front side.

▸ **TIP**

Avoid digging or plowing between the layers of fabric. You're more likely to cut your fabric that way.

Pam vs. The Machine. "I had to re-thread my old machine no fewer than 50 times during one project and I grew extremely frustrated. It was a lesson in knowing when to step away from the machine, take a break, and come back to it. Rome wasn't built in a day and, for me, neither was that project!"
—PAM

Cutting 101

▸ **Measure Twice, Cut Once**

Cutting is the first step in getting a professional look to your project. It's also the one area that my students were most nervous to try on their own. It takes a bit to get the hang of rotary cutting and reading the markings on acrylic rulers, but the time spent practicing will pay off and you'll be much more confident before you know it. Incorrectly cut fabric will set you on the wrong path from the start, so take your time and remember the #1 cutting rule: "measure twice, cut once."

ROTARY CUTTING BASICS

The vast majority of projects in this book can be cut using a rotary cutter, a self-healing mat, and acrylic rulers. Practice with scrap fabric or inexpensive muslin if you're nervous about cutting your precious and pretty project fabric. Keep these tips in mind as you cut:

▸ Always cut from a standing position in order to get the most leverage behind each cut.

▸ Use the rotary cutter with the same hand you use to write.

▸ Cut by moving the rotary cutter away from your body, sliding the blade along the edge of the ruler.

▸ Always, always, always close the blade on your rotary cutter when you're not using it! One cut of your finger and you'll never forget this rule. Choose a self-retracting blade if you think you'll be forgetful.

▸ When you find yourself having to push on the rotary cutter to get it to cut the fabric, it's time to replace the dull blade. Always buy replacement blades from the same manufacturer.

▸ Line up the fabric (or the fold of the fabric) along a horizontal line nearest you on the cutting mat.

Selvages will be together at the upper edge of the mat.

▸ Place the ruler on the fabric. Be sure the ruler is lined up with the same vertical measurement markings at both the top and bottom of the cutting mat.

▸ Square up the cut edge of the fabric. It's not always square when you bring it home from the store. Do this by trimming a small strip of fabric from fold to selvage.

▸ Press firmly on the ruler with one hand. Keep those fingers far from the cutting edge. Safety first!

▸ When a pattern, such as that for the My First Quilt project, calls for a "width of fabric" cut, often abbreviated as WOF, you'll cut vertically from the fold to the selvage edges for a full selvage-to-selvage strip of fabric.

▸ If desired, flip the position of your mat, so the straight cut edge is now on the opposite side of your body. Use the markings on the ruler to cut the desired size piece of fabric.

PATTERN CUTTING BASICS

This book doesn't dive into garment sewing, so should you wish try your hand at sewing clothing, I recommend checking the titles referenced in the Resources section for some excellent garment sewing books. For the purposes of the projects in this book, use these tips for successful cutting of each fabric piece:

▸ Copy the template sheet at 100% or trace the template onto freezer paper. (See Freezer Paper Pattern Pieces at right.) Cut out the template.

▸ Place the template on fabric, paying attention to any grainline markings (as in garment sewing) and pin in place. Any arrows should go with the grainline/length of the fabric (parallel to

FREEZER PAPER PATTERN PIECES

Yes, that's right. The freezer paper that you get at the grocery store! Freezer paper is my favorite pattern piece trick. Trace the pattern piece with the shiny side of the freezer paper down, including any grainline marks or notches. Cut the traced template and iron it directly to the fabric. No pinning required! Cut around the template and peel the paper right off. You can even reuse it multiple times! Try it with the Carry-All Clutch and Tech Case. It's a great trick for using with garment patterns in order to preserve all the sizes on the original pattern tissue.

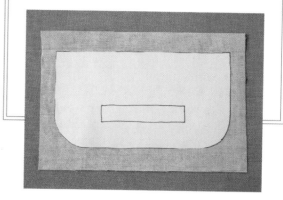

selvages). If a pattern calls for cutting two of a piece, simply pin the pattern piece to a double thickness of fabric and pay attention to how the patterns says right sides of the fabric should be positioned.

▸ Cut at the edge of the pattern piece, using dressmaker shears. A rotary cutter and acrylic ruler can be used for straight edges, if desired.

▸ Transfer any markings such as darts, pivot points, notches, or buttonholes to the wrong side of the fabric.

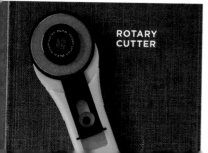

ROTARY CUTTER

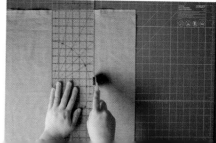

CLIPPING CORNERS

CLIPPING CURVES

FUSSY CUTTING

CLIPPING CORNERS AND CURVES

When cutting outside corners, cut at an angle to allow space for the fabric to form a point when you turn it right side out. Taper the corners by trimming away along both sides of the corner. Interior corners should be clipped up to but not into the stitching line.

Cutting outer (convex) curves involves clipping V-shaped notches to avoid bulk in the seam when turned right side out. Inner (concave) curves need only snips up to the stitch line, allowing the curve to have some give as the project is turned right side out. In both cases, be sure to avoid clipping the stitch line!

FUSSY CUTTING

You may want to cut around a specific image from a printed fabric. In this instance, you'll want to fussy cut the fabric (cut around the exact spot on the fabric you want). Clear acrylic rulers are perfect for this, as they allow you to see what you're cutting. Place painter's tape on the ruler, creating a frame. Keep in mind that fussy cutting does use up more fabric than usual.

GENERAL TIPS

▸ Pay attention to directional fabrics: do you want those stripes going up and down or left to right?

▸ Always iron fabric prior to cutting. You can still fold the fabric and cut along the length, but you want to remove any wrinkles before cutting.

▸ Rotary supplies go together. Never use a rotary cutter without a self-healing mat. (Yikes!)

▸ Using your rotary cutter on paper will dull the blade.

▸ Larger rotary cutting blades (60mm) are best for thick fabrics and straight lines. Smaller rotary cutters (28mm) are great for cutting curves.

Pressing 101

Pressing is a step many beginners want to skip over to get on with the sewing. Don't be tempted to do this! Pressing is often what makes the difference between handmade and homemade in the final appearance of your project. Done correctly, you'll often press between each step of your project. Not only does pressing make the fabric look better; it also makes the pieces sew together much more easily.

IRONING VS. PRESSING

Pressing in sewing is much different than ironing your favorite dress shirt. Pressing means lifting and lowering the iron repeatedly over the surface of the fabric, while ironing means moving back and forth. In order to keep fabric from shifting and becoming otherwise distorted, we press in sewing.

SETTING A SEAM

Setting a seam means to meld the thread with the fabric for a flat seam. First, press the seam flat, just as it looks coming off the machine, then press open or to one side as instructed. As a final step, flip the project over and press with the right side up.

TO STEAM OR NOT TO STEAM?

This is a hot button topic in the world of sewing and quilting! Steam fans argue that it makes for a much more flat fabric or seam, while the No Steam Team says that the added water in steam warps fabric. I say try them both.

PRESSING AND INTERFACING

Use a press cloth or scrap both beneath and above your project to protect your ironing surface and your iron from potential adhesive residue. Keep a spray bottle of water handy. If interfacing doesn't seem to be fusing, spray the press cloth with a light mist of water, then press.

PRESSING IN TIGHT QUARTERS

In projects such as the Tech Case or the Pleated Purse, pressing side seams open can be tricky. Use a seam roll or a tightly rolled towel to insert beneath the seam. You'll be able open the seam without adding a crease elsewhere in the project.

SPRAY STARCH

People love it or hate it. I happen to love it and use Mary Ellen's Best Press on almost all my projects, especially seams in quilts. See the difference it made here on the right seam in the photo below? Keep in mind that since spraying starch onto a project adds moisture to the fabric, you definitely want to press instead of iron.

IRONED SEAM WITHOUT STARCH

IRONED SEAM WITH STARCH

FINGER PRESSING

Finger pressing won't give you the nice crisp results that using an iron provides, but it works in a pinch if you need to. To finger press, simply run your fingernail along the length of a seam being careful not to distort the fabric. I use this trick when an iron won't fit, like when I'm joining the two ends of binding on a project.

SETTING A SEAM

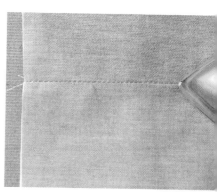

Hand Sewing

Hand sewing is stitching using its most basic elements: needle and thread. Often used to complete the finishing details on a project, such as binding a quilt or tacking down a lining in a bag, hand sewing is a skill you'll want to hone. Luckily it doesn't take much time to get the hang of sewing this way. Let's get going!

THREADING A NEEDLE

Pull thread from the spool and clip the end to keep a crisp end for inserting into the eye of the needle. As for how much thread to use, 18"-24" is a good length. Using thread that is longer than your arm usually ends in tangles, twists, and knots. Insert the thread into the eye of the needle, using a needle threader if you have difficulty. Decide if you want to sew with a single or double thickness of thread. For a double thickness, pull the thread tails even with each other.

TYING A KNOT

You've got two options. The standard and easy way: make a small loop near the end of the thread and insert the tail through, pulling to tighten it. Then there's the amazing quilter's knot! Start with a threaded needle. With your right hand, pinch the end of the tail against the eye end of the needle. With your left hand, tightly wind the thread around the needle three or four times, close to your thumb. Winding more will make a larger knot. Carefully inch your pinched fingers over the wrapped thread, which is about to become the knot. With your left hand, pull the needle so the wrapped thread moves over the eye of the needle and down the length of thread. Your right hand will keep pinching the wrapped thread the whole time. A perfect knot will remain at the end of your thread!

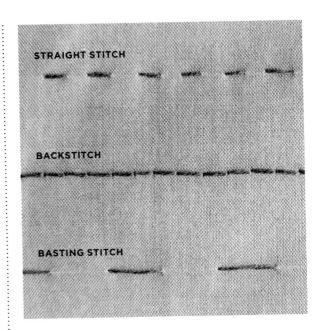

BASIC STITCHES

Straight Stitch

The most basic of stitches, the straight stitch is also called the running stitch. It involves the needle going up or down through the fabric with each stitch, keeping all stitches the same length. The smaller and closer the stitches are, the stronger the seam.

Backstitch

In this stitch, you'll bring the needle up through the fabric and then reenter the fabric one stitch length in reverse. Then bring the needle up two stitch lengths forward. Continue this pattern for a strong stitching line.

Basting Stitch

A variation of the straight stitch, basting is done to temporarily join fabrics. Very large stitches are taken, allowing them to be easily removed.

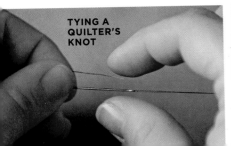

TYING A QUILTER'S KNOT

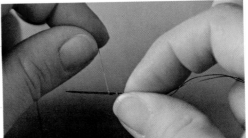

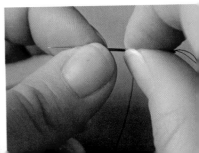

CLEANING

OILING

GENERAL TIPS

▶ Using beeswax for thread or a thread conditioner, such as Thread Heaven, greatly reduces the likelihood of twists and knots as you're sewing. Just run your thread over the wax using your thumb to hold it in place.

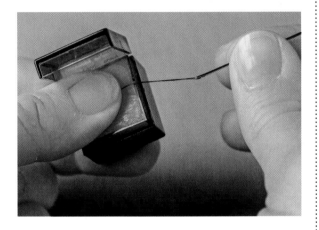

▶ A single thickness of thread will be hidden more easily. Use double thread for strength: buttons, bindings, etc.

▶ Insert a folded piece of thread into a needle to create a quadruple thickness perfect for sewing buttons on in a speedy manner.

▶ Always start stitches from the wrong side of the fabric, which allows you to hide your knot.

▶ Tie off or knot your stitches on the back side of your project when you come to the end of a line. Sew a small backstitch, with the needle passing through the loop, to form a knot.

▶ Embroidery floss can be used to add a decorative flourish to a project. Be sure to use a needle with a larger eye.

Machine Maintenance

▶ Keep Your Machine in Top Shape

Get into the habit of cleaning, oiling, and changing the needle on your machine all at the same time. It's a powerful trifecta. Much like taking care of a car, your machine will hum along for years with a little routine maintenance. How often to clean depends on how often you sew. The recommendation is to clean after every few projects. If I'm using felt, flannel, or batting in a project, I'll clean more often.

CLEANING

Cleaning your machine should be one of the first skills you learn. Lint builds up quickly, depending on fabrics types you use most often, and can cause all kinds of problems in the bobbin housing.

Start by unplugging your machine. Safety first! Follow along in your manual, but in general you will remove the throatplate and presser foot as well as the free arm, bobbin, and bobbin holder or case. Brush and wipe the bobbin holder with a soft cloth or machine cleaning brush. Brush and remove lint from the inside of the machine, at the area called the hook race. For any large tricky-to-grab pieces of lint, you may need to use a pair of tweezers. Clean around the feed dogs, too. Oil your machine here, if needed, before replacing everything you removed.

Replace your needle while the presser foot is removed.

OILING

If your manual is unclear, ask your local dealer for information on your specific model. Don't skip this step! It's actually quite simple and is vital to a well operating machine. If your machine sounds loud as it sews, chances are it could use a little oil. Look for small tubes of sewing machine oil at your dealer or fabric store. After oiling, run the machine for a few seconds without thread or fabric to get the oil moving around, and then sew a few seams on scrap fabric to avoid any potential oil spots on your actual projects.

CHANGING THE NEEDLE

Change your needle after every large project (like a bag or quilt) or after roughly eight hours of sewing. Needles dull faster than you'd expect and are very inexpensive to replace. Never underestimate the difference a new needle can make. Be sure your machine is off, then loosen the screw on the needle bar. Slide out the old needle and dispose of it safely. Insert the new needle with the flat side of the needle top facing away from you and tighten the screw. Use the handwheel to advance the needle, confirming that everything is working properly.

GENERAL TIPS

▸ Take your machine in for service once a year. Much like a multi-point check on your car, a machine tune-up keeps things running and often catches small problems before they become large problems.

▸ Never used compressed air when cleaning your machine.

▸ When you're not using your machine, use a hardshell or fabric cover to protect it from dust, which is not a friend to sewing machines and their moving parts.

Your Sewing Studio

▸ Setting Up a Sewing Space

Carving out a place that is yours for sewing is so important — be it a room just for your new craft or simply the dining room table. For the purposes of this book, we'll work with the assumption that you'll be sewing in a room that pulls double duty, a bedroom or dining room or basement. The square footage isn't the most important part. It's the way you set up the space that makes it ultra-functional and gets you more sewing time when you're ready to create. Let's look at some ideas!

THE TABLE

Use the sturdiest table you can find. No card tables allowed! A lightweight table will cause your machine to bounce around when sewing. No one likes to sew a moving target.

Use a height-adjustable office chair with great back support. You don't want to be hunched over or straining to reach the machine. These chairs are also great for pivoting between sewing, cutting, and pressing stations.

Good lighting is vital. Dim lights will not only hurt your eyes; they can lead to poor craftsmanship if you can't see what you're working on. Natural light is best for daytime sewing, but if you get your sewing time in at night, adjustable tabletop lights are a huge help. Choose a task lamp with a bulb that mimics natural light if possible.

When it comes to cutting, counter height is best for your back. A standard table can be made higher with plastic bed risers.

THE TOOLKIT

An industrial toolbox, tackle box, or cosmetics case makes a perfect modern-day sewing box! Tiered trays extend to display your thread, seam ripper, machine accessories, and other favorite notions. The handle is perfect for toting to class and a latch means your gear won't spill everywhere.

THE STORAGE

▸ Look for a rolling kitchen cart that can be easily filled and tucked away into a nearby closet or corner. The IKEA Raskög cart shown here is a favorite among crafters.

- Always stash your cutting mat flat. *Always*. Never lean it against a wall or in the back of a hot car. If it can't be left on a table, store it under a bed or couch.

- An over-the-door or tabletop ironing board works well and conceals easily.

- Thread stands can be used on a tabletop or mounted on a wall for some great colorful decor!

THE FABRIC

When you first start, your fabric stash will be slim. Eventually, you'll start to amass some scraps from each project. You'll want to protect your fabric stash — no matter the size. Avoid direct sunlight and dust. Dresser drawers or storage bins with clear drawers are good choices.

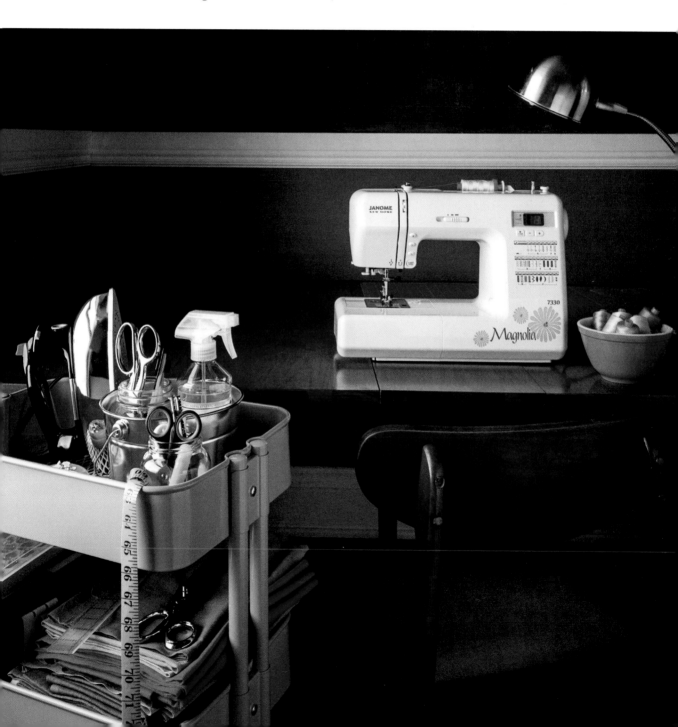

The Help Desk

▸ Troubleshooting

Face it. Problems are going to happen. Most likely it will be a problem with the stitch quality, but these are common and can be solved on your own with a little time and tinkering.

Mark this section for frequent reference, as these troubleshooting skills are important to learn. It's also good to know when to walk away. If needed, give yourself a break and then come back to the machine.

The good news is that the vast majority of problems can be solved by simply changing to a new needle, reinserting the bobbin, re-threading the machine, or adjusting the thread tension.

WHAT DO I DO IF ...

The thread keeps breaking

Re-thread upper thread from the beginning and don't miss any thread guides. Be sure your thread and needle are the right thickness for the fabric you are using. Check to be sure thread tension isn't too tight. Does the eye of the needle have a burr that is catching on the thread?

The bobbin is having problems

Make sure the bobbin is inserted properly and that the bobbin case is clean of lint or any extra threads. Be sure the thread comes off the bobbin in the correct direction. Be sure the bobbin itself is threaded correctly, that the wound thread is not loose and spongy.

I'm getting skipped stitches

Check the needle. Is it the right size or is it damaged? Be sure the bobbin has plenty of thread. Be sure the take-up lever is threaded.

My needle breaks

Be sure your needle is large enough for the thickness of your fabric. Check to be sure the needle is inserted all the way and check the bobbin case for proper insertion. Turn the handwheel and watch the needle near the presser foot. Is the needle hitting the foot? If so, switch to the presser foot appropriate for your stitch.

There's a hole in my seam

Your seam allowance probably isn't wide enough, which makes for a weak seam or, in your case, a seam with a hole! Seam rip the stitches in that area, re-pin, and sew the correct seam allowance.

The bottom of my seam is a giant mess

Re-thread the machine and check the upper thread tension. See Thread Tension 101, below.

The fabrics aren't the same length and I ended up with a big pucker

This happens if fabrics weren't cut accurately or if a bias edge has stretched. You need to "ease" the seam to prevent puckers. You may need to rip out some of the seam to get enough fabric to ease the excess. Pin the two lengths at the centers, then work to split the difference with more pins at center points until the area has pins every ½" or so. Sew with the larger (wrinkly) piece down- often the feed dogs can aid in easing the excess. Meanwhile, stretch the shorter piece ever so slightly to help the seam come out even.

The fabric keeps puckering along the seam

Try a smaller stitch length, such as 2.0mm stitch length. Upper tension may be incorrect. Be sure the bobbin and top thread are the same thickness. The thread may be too thick or heavy for the fabric.

My needle comes unthreaded

Be sure you're giving yourself plenty of thread tail to start. If you trim the thread too close to the presser foot, the next seam you sew will pull that short thread right out of the needle. Be sure the take-up lever is fully raised before starting the seam.

My first stitches on any seam end in tangles

Try a using a fabric leader scrap (see page 58), or simply hold both threads to the back of the machine as you start the seam.

The needle won't move

If you have a manual machine and just filled a bobbin, push in on the handwheel to engage it. Be sure the presser foot is down.

My machine is making loud noises

Clean your machine and oil it if necessary. The needle may be bent and need replacing. Be sure the presser foot is installed properly.

The fabric isn't moving under the presser foot

Check the feed dogs to be sure they are up. Be sure the presser foot is down and has enough pressure and that the fabric isn't too thick to grab. If the fabric is thick, start your seam a bit forward on the fabric and reverse stitch first, then stitch forward — or try using a fabric leader (see page 58).

My interfacing won't stick

Use a mist of water from a spray bottle or a damp press cloth. Try turning the project over and iron with the right side of the fabric on top.

THREAD TENSION 101

What is thread tension? Proper thread tension means that the upper thread and bobbin thread meet in the middle of the fabric and stitches look identical on both sides. Tension is controlled by the dial on the upper thread path, which is adjusted to either tighten or loosen the machine's grip on the upper thread.

If you have a problem with stitches on one side of the fabric, the problem is with the thread on the *opposite* side. For example, loops and knots on the bottom mean your upper thread has a problem. Picture the threads playing a game of tug-of-war. You want the tugging to be equally strong on both sides. If the top thread is too loose (a weak tug-of-war player), the bobbin will pull too much upper thread through and cause loops and problems on the underside. In that instance, increase the number on the tension dial. Typically a minor thread tension adjustment will do the trick. The middle tension settings from 3 to 5 are usually the sweet spot. (The dial should not need to be adjusted beyond this except when sewing on especially thin, slippery, or thick fabrics.) Having said that, before you change anything, pull on both threads to be sure one is not stuck coming off the spool or bobbin, then try simply removing the spool and bobbin and re-threading.

THE
PROJECTS

SPEEDY PILLOWCASE

The quintessential beginner project! This pillowcase teaches more skills than you think and is easy to personalize with fabric choices. You'll impress your friends and family when you show off the professional finish! We will warn you though … you will want to make one for every bed in your house! Try making these from luxurious voile for the summer or cozy flannel for the winter.

Features: French seams inside, no raw edges exposed, quick to make

Finished size: 20″ x 30″

Fabric: Choose quilting cottons, flannel, or voile.

GATHER
⅞ yard main fabric
⅜ yard cuff fabric

CUT
27″ x 41″ from main fabric
9″ x 41″ from cuff fabric

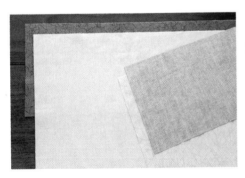

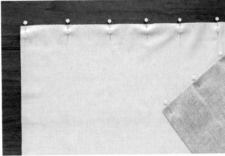

1. Lay cuff fabric right side up on work surface. Position main fabric on top of cuff fabric, wrong side up. Match one 41″ edge of the main fabric with one 41″ edge of the cuff fabric.

2. Pin along length of matched edge. These pins are temporary.

▶ HOW TO PIN

Insert pins into the fabric perpendicular to the raw edge. I suggest pinning each end first, then pin at the center. Continue splitting the difference and pinning in the center of two pins until you have pins every 3" to 4". I used ten pins when sewing my pillowcase cuff.

"I remember feeling this great sense of accomplishment when I finished this project. I remember thinking, 'If this tube comes out as a pillowcase, I will be utterly amazed.' I've never even heard of a French seam before Shea told us about it, but I made sure I told everyone I just did it!"

—CHRISTINE

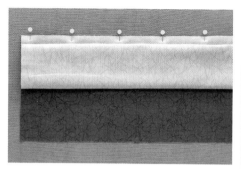 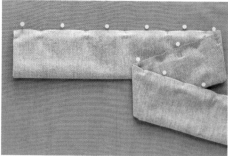

3. Roll up bottom edge of main fabric. Continue rolling main fabric until it is positioned in middle of cuff fabric.

4. Pick up bottom edge of cuff fabric. Bring over roll of main fabric and match to raw edge at top of work surface. Re-pin layers along 41" edge. Three layers will be pinned: cuff, main fabric, and cuff. It looks crazy, but I promise this will work!

5. Sew along raw edges using ½" seam allowance, backstitching at each end. Remember to pull out each pin before you sew over it. Fabric will form a tube.

6. Pull out main fabric from one side of tube. Cuff will now be right side out.

7. Press seam toward cuff.

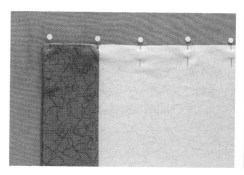

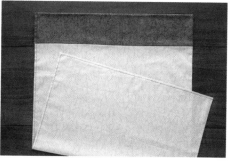

8. Fold pillowcase in half, wrong sides of main fabric together. Match raw edges and pin where cuff meets main fabric. Pin along both raw edges. Don't worry! Wrong sides together is correct. Promise! You're about to sew a French seam, which will hide all raw edges.

9. Sew both raw edges, using ¼" seam allowance. Don't forget to pull those pins!

PIVOT AT CORNERS LIKE A PRO!

Here's how: When you are ¼" from the corner, stop with the needle down. Raise the presser foot and pivot the fabric to the next edge. Lower the presser foot and continue sewing the next edge.

EXTRA CREDIT

Add extra detail to your pillowcase by sewing a trim piece at the cuff. This is called a flange. You'll need ⅛ yard of coordinating fabric. Cut a 1½''' x 41'' strip. Fold and press in half along length of strip, wrong sides together. Pin along one 41'' edge of main fabric, right sides together and raw edges aligned. Don't be shy with the pins! Sew using ¼'' seam allowance. Proceed with pillowcase instructions, starting at Step 1. Trim will be sandwiched between cuff and main fabric when pinning at Step 2. Sew slowly near cuff seam at Steps 8 and 9, as seam will be quite thick.

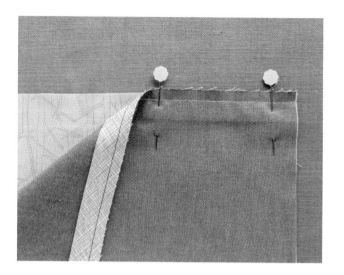

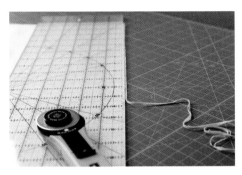

10. Trim seam allowance to ⅛″.

11. Turn pillowcase inside out. Press seam allowance flat, using your fingers to wiggle the seam as flat as possible.

12. Sew along both the side and bottom again, using ¼″ seam allowance. Backstitch at both ends and pivot at the corner.

13. Turn pillowcase right side out. There! Aren't you so impressed with yourself?

"I loved going home with a finished product! The fancy French seam that we learned was also fun! You look at products that other people make, and you think to yourself, 'I could never do that!' Until you do! And it's so cool to learn those tricks to making things look far more fancy than they really are!"

—CALI

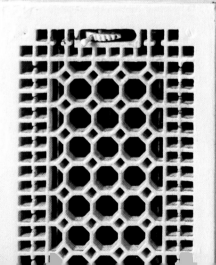

LINED DRAWSTRING BAG

Designed by
Jeni Baker

Jeni's design for this drawstring bag became an instant favorite with my School of Sewing students. Equally great for holding crayons and toy cars or packing cords and battery chargers for trips, it is sure to become a favorite of yours, too. I skip the store-bought gift bags and fill these with treats for teacher gifts each year. I bet you can't make just one!

Features: Easy-to-close drawstring, fully lined, boxed corners

Finished size: 10″ x 7″

Fabric: Choose quilting cottons in prints or solids.

GATHER
3 fat quarters

⅛ yard drawstring fabric OR 2 yards grosgrain ribbon or twill tape

Fabric marking pen

Large safety pin

Edgestitch presser foot (optional)

CUT
(2) 9″ x 10½″ from exterior main fabric

(2) 4″ x 10½″ from exterior accent fabric

(2) 12½″ x 10½″ from interior fabric

(2) 2″ x 32″ from drawstring fabric OR (2) 32″ of ribbon/twill tape

Use ¼″ seam allowance unless otherwise noted.

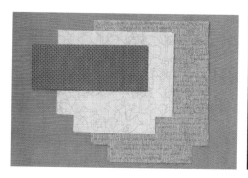

1. Cut a 1½″ square from two bottom corners of both interior pieces and both main exterior pieces. The bottom of each piece should now measure 10½″. These will make your boxed corners later.

2. Arrange pieces in this order, aligning all 10½″ edges: interior, exterior accent, exterior main, exterior main, exterior accent, interior. Be sure any directional prints are arranged with the top of the print facing out, toward interior pieces. Ensure all corner cutouts are oriented properly.

▶ **TIP**
To help yourself remember to leave openings like this unsewn, place two pins next to each other for a visual reminder as you sew.

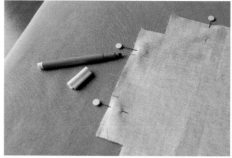

3. Working down the row of fabrics, sew each piece to the next along 10½" sides, creating one long strip. Backstitch at start and stop of each seam. Press seams open.

4. Fold sewn strip in half, right sides together, matching interior ends. Pin along raw edges, leaving a 3" space open at the center of the open end.

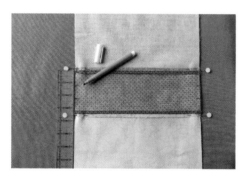

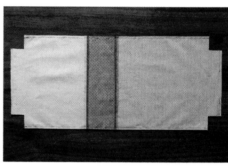

5. Mark a 1" opening in the center of the accent fabric piece by measuring 1¼" in from each seam. Repeat for remaining side. Leave these sections unsewn, creating an opening for the drawstrings.

6. Sew along three sides. Leave the corner cutouts, openings at the accent pieces, and opening at bottom of the interior un-sewn.

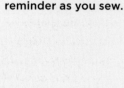

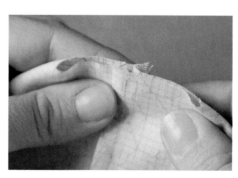

7. Create boxed corners by pinching open corner cutouts and bringing seams together in middle. Pin. Sew corner closed, backstitching at each end. Repeat for remaining three corners.

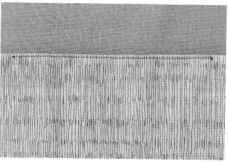

8. Turn bag right side out, pulling fabric gently through the 3″ opening in interior. Carefully push out corners.

9. Press the interior opening under ¼″ and stitch closed with ⅛″ seam allowance.

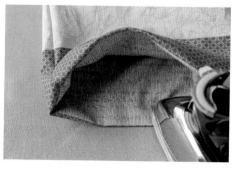

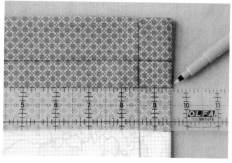

10. Nestle interior inside the exterior fabric. Press along top edge for polished finish.

11. Find the 1″ openings on each exterior accent piece. Mark horizontal lines 1¼″ from top and from bottom seams of accent piece. Lines will meet at top and bottom of opening. Use acrylic ruler to extend lines around entire bag.

"This was a big jump from the pillowcase. I learned to rotary cut, which was sort of scary at first. Following more complex steps was a huge stress point, but then seeing it all come together was awesome. This one made me feel like if I can do this, I can do so many projects."

—MIMI

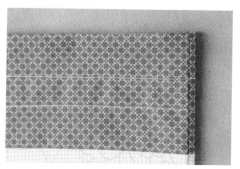

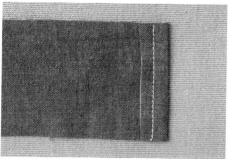

12. Sew all the way around accent piece on marked lines, starting at side seam and backstitching at start and stop. This creates the casing for the drawstring. Use the free arm feature on your machine, if preferred (see Free Arm, p. 26).

13. If you are using ribbon or twill tape for the drawstring, skip to Step 18. If you are using fabric: Fold and press short ends of drawstring fabric ¼″ to wrong side. Topstitch to secure.

14. Fold drawstring fabric in half lengthwise, wrong sides together. Press.

15. Unfold. Bring raw edges to center crease from Step 14. Press.

16. Fold in half again and press, encasing raw edges.

17. Edgestitch along open edge to close. Repeat with remaining drawstring. If your machine has trouble grabbing the edge of the drawstring to start, use a fabric leader (see page 58).

WHAT IS EDGESTITCHING?

At times decorative and other times a functional stitch, an edgestitch is typically used in two main ways: sewing parallel to a seam at a distance of ⅛" or ⅟₁₆", or sewing along an opening in a lining (and, as in this case, a drawstring) to close it. A ditch or edgestitching presser foot is incredibly useful for consistently maintaining that small seam allowance. You'll use this stitch often in our projects, so there's plenty of opportunity to practice it.

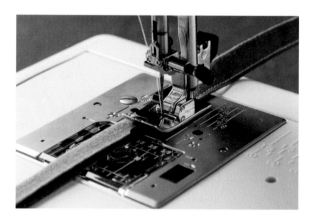

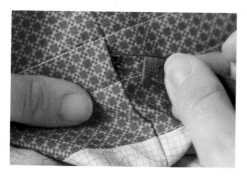

18. Attach safety pin to one end of the fabric drawstring or ribbon. Insert safety pin into one of side openings. The safety pin acts as a bodkin, helping you thread the drawstring through the casing.

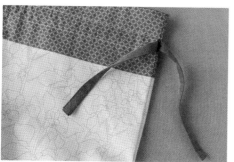

19. Push safety pin through casing, passing the other opening and pulling all the way back around and out the first opening.

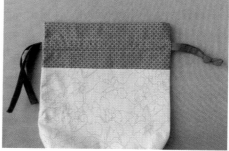

20. Even out ends and tie together in a tight knot. Repeat with remaining drawstring, starting at opposite side opening.

JENI BAKER spends most of her time quilting, blogging, and knitting. She designs retro-inspired fabric collections, self-publishes modern quilting patterns, and teaches intermediate sewing locally in Wisconsin. Find her blog at In Color Order, www.incolororder.com.

SIMPLE STRINGS APRON

These aprons have been a favorite in my family for nearly a decade. One quick tug on the strings and the apron adjusts easily to fit everyone, no matter the height or size. Choose to make yours from one fabric or two for added spunk. You will find a smaller version in the Extra Credit if a special child in your life wants one, too!

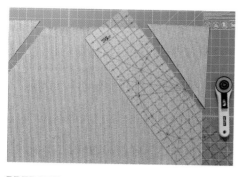

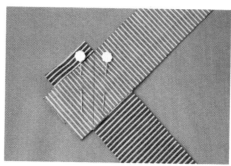

PREPARE

Mark a point on main apron 9½″ down from top left corner, along 28″ length. Mark a point 7½″ over from top corner along 26″ width. Draw line connecting these points and trim off triangle. Repeat with right side of apron panel. Avoid handling this angled edge too much in order to prevent bias edges from stretching.

APRON STRINGS

1. Trim off selvages from string strips. Sew string strips together. With right sides together, sew ends at 45-degree angle.

2. Trim seam allowance to ¼″. Press seam open. Add remaining strip in the same manner.

Features: Topstitching, all-in-one adjustable strings, divided pocket

Finished size: 24″ x 26″long

Fabric: Choose washable home decor fabrics or quilting cottons.

GATHER
1 yard for main apron body

½ yard for pocket and strings

Fabric marking pen

Safety pin or bodkin

Sheet of cardstock

Edgestitch presser foot (optional)

1″ Bias tape maker (optional)

If you plan to make more than one apron, a bias tape maker (page 156) can be a great tool to have. It really speeds up the apron string pressing steps! Cut string strips 1⅞″ wide instead of 2″ if using this shortcut.

CUT
26″ wide x 28″ long for main apron

(3) 2″ x width of fabric strips for strings

25″ wide x 11″ long for pocket

If using fabrics with a strong directional print, be sure the print is placed along the width before cutting to size.

If you like a longer apron, cut the main panel 34″ long and omit the pocket, hemming the lower edge by ¼″ then ½″ before sewing.

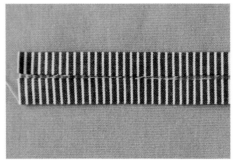

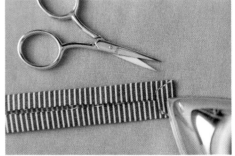

3. Fold strip in half lengthwise. Press. Open strip and fold in both long sides to meet at pressed center.

If using the bias tape maker, skip Step 3. Instead, follow the directions from the manufacturer for pressing with the bias tape maker.

4. Clip corners, then tuck and fold in raw edge at both ends of strip.

▶ **TIP**
In Step 5 use fabric scrap as a leader (see page 58) to guide fabric for topstitching. An edgestitching presser foot is helpful here.

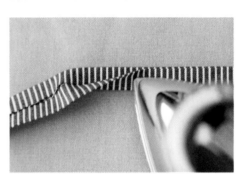

5. Fold strip in half lengthwise again. Press.

6. Topstitch ⅛'' from edge to close.

APRON PANEL
7. Fold in sides of apron ½'' to wrong side. Press. Fold in another ½''. Press and topstitch as close as possible to inner edge.

8. Fold in top edge of apron ½'' to wrong side and press. Fold in another 1¼'' and press.

HEM PAPER PRESSING GUIDES

These are helpful for this project or any time a straight edge needs to be hemmed. For this project, from cardstock cut ½″ strips and 1¼″ strips. Place on wrong side of fabric. Fold over raw edge of fabric to meet inside edge of hem paper. Press fabric with paper in place. Slide hem paper along length of hem and repeat pressing to complete rest of hemming.

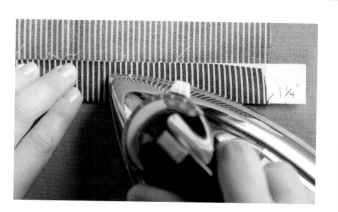

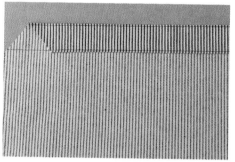

9. Topstitch ⅛″ from both inner and outer edges of the fold. The edgestitch presser foot is helpful here.

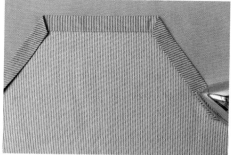

10. Fold in angled edges of apron ½″ to wrong side and press. Fold in another 1¼″ and press.

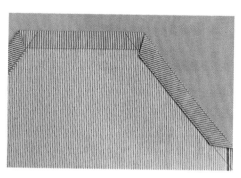

11. Topstitch ⅛″ from both inner and outer edges of folds. Extend stitches to top and side edges of apron for a clean stitching line on apron front. To make these stitches easier, draw guidelines with a fabric marking pen and straight edge. The topstitching creates a casing, which allows you to thread the apron strings through.

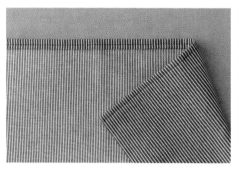

POCKET

12. Fold ½″ on top edge of pocket panel to wrong side. Fold in another ½″ and press. Topstitch closed ¼″ at inner edge. This will become the top of the pocket.

13. Fold short edges ½″ to wrong side and press.

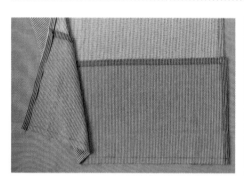

14. Pin right side of pocket and wrong side of apron together along bottom edge. Lengths should match. If not, fold in sides of pocket more to adjust. Sew unfinished long edge of pocket to the apron using ½″ seam allowance.

15. Press seam toward apron. Fold pocket up and over to the right side of apron. Wrong side of pocket will lay on right side of apron. Press bottom edge, working the seam flat with your fingers.

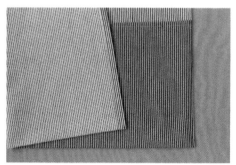

16. Pin pocket along both sides. Topstitch ⅛″ from outer edge of the sides, starting at bottom and reinforcing top corners of pocket with extra stitching.

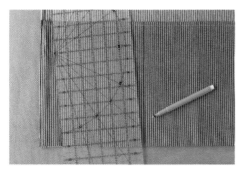 

17. Mark pocket along top and bottom 8″ from each side. Using fabric marking pen, draw two vertical lines connecting points. Sew two straight seams connecting your marks to make three sections. Start at bottom and reinforce top of each section.

18. Using a safety pin, thread string through apron casing. Begin at one side, travel up to the neck area, then down the remaining side.

EXTRA CREDIT

Use the following pattern modifications to make a kid-size version, perfect for art projects or helping in the kitchen. Gather ¾ yard of main fabric and ½ yard for the pocket and strings. Finished size: 18″ wide x 21″ long

Cut 20″ wide x 23″ long rectangle for main apron, 19″ x 9″ rectangle for pocket, and (2) 2″ x width of fabric strips for the string. Mark main apron panel as in instructions above, marking a point 6½″ down from top corners and on top edge 5″ in from top corners. Follow Steps 1–16, using the same seam allowances as the regular apron. At Step 17, mark the pocket along the top and bottom edges at center and sew one line of stitches to create two pockets before continuing with the instructions.

RUFFLED WRISTLET KEY FOB

Designed by
Alex Ledgerwood

My friend Alex designed this ultra-useful project. After I made and started using my own, I noticed how many people would ask about it. It did not take long for this to become my go-to gift! My friends, neighbors, family, and my children's teachers have all been recipients. Selecting it as a project for our School of Sewing was a no-brainer — the group got to make these and walk out the door with them already in use!

Features: Gathered ruffle, topstitching, sturdy interfacing, D-ring hardware

Finished size: 7″ x 1½″

Fabric: Choose cotton prints or solids. Avoid home decor fabrics.

GATHER
¼ yard strap fabric

2½″ x 22″ strip ruffle fabric

¼ yard fusible interfacing (such as Pellon 911FF fusible featherweight)

1¼″ D-ring

Zipper presser foot

Safety pin

Four key fobs can be made from only two fat quarters!

CUT
5″ x 13″ for strap

2½″ x 22″ for ruffle

5″ x 12″ fusible interfacing

1. Fuse interfacing to wrong side of strap fabric, centering along length. Fabric will show ½″ on each short end.

2. Fold ruffle strip in half, right sides together, to form a long narrow strip. Sew ruffle's raw edges together with a ¼″ seam along long edge, backstitching at each end.

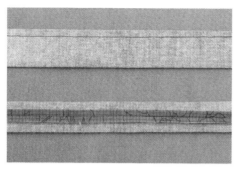

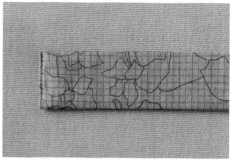

3. Press seam open, positioning in the center of the strip.

4. Insert safety pin into one layer of fabric at end of tube. Push safety pin through tube to turn right side out.

▶ **TIP**
Use a fabric leader (see page 58) if topstitching in Step 5 is difficult.

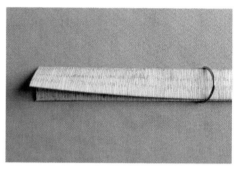

5. Press so that seam is in center of strip. Turn raw edges inside tube by ¼″ and topstitch along narrow ends.

6. Press strap fabric in half lengthwise, wrong sides together. Open and fold raw edges toward center crease. Press. Fold along length again and press. The fabric will now be folded in quarters to form a 1¼″ strip.

7. Slip the D-ring onto strip.

"When I was trying to make the ruffle, my thread kept breaking because I was rushing and not taking my time. Lesson 1: take your time. Lesson 2: there's no such thing as a perfect ruffle!"

—PAM

8. Unfold the two ends of strip. Line up raw edges, right sides together. Pin. Sew a ¼″ seam. Press seam open.

9. Refold strap to form a circle.

10. Topstitch along both sides of circle, keeping D-ring out of the way. Be sure topstitching on open edge catches lower fold.

If your machine has a free arm (page 26), this is an excellent place to use it!

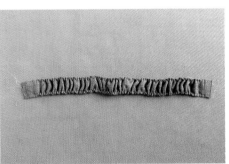

11. Change stitch length to longest setting, often called a basting stitch (page 59). Create the ruffle by using a basting stitch on both sides of the ruffle, ⅛″ from each edge. Leave thread tails 2″ to 3″ in length at both ends of stitching. Do not backstitch at either end.

12. Pull gently on bobbin (bottom) thread to ruffle the fabric until the ruffle is 11″ long. Try to evenly distribute fabric along the length of the strip.

"While sewing down the ruffles, I had to get over the worry of sewing fabric that was bunched up and not smooth. I was so concerned that I was doing something wrong and ended up flattening a section. After that, I made sure to just let it be bunched up and kept on sewing."

—AMY

▶ TIP

Alternate pulling threads from both ends of the ruffle to avoid thread breakage. If threads do snap, simply pull out the basting stitches and re-sew. Or, try starting basting stitches at the center of the ruffle and sewing to each end. This allows for a smaller work area.

13. Find center of ruffle and pin to center of strap, opposite the strap seam. Place each ruffle end 1" to 1½" from seam on strap. Pin along ruffle. Return stitch length to standard setting. Sew ruffle to strap, sewing down center of strip, backstitching at each end.

14. Trim threads and remove basting stitches using seam ripper (see Seam Ripping 101, page 60.)

15. Place D-ring so it lines up with seam on strap. With D-ring in the fold, sew ¼" to ¾" from D-ring, depending on how big you'd like wristlet loop to be. Use zipper foot to sew near D-ring.

16. Hook your keys onto your new ruffled wristlet key fob with a split circle ring.

EXTRA CREDIT

Swap the ruffle for a flat strip of fabric. Keep cutting instructions the same, substituting a 1½" x 13" strip for the ruffle. Fold in half along length, wrong sides together. Unfold and bring both raw edges to center fold, wrong sides together, along length. Center along length of one of the middle fourths of the strap after completing Step 4, being sure to pin through only one layer of the strap. Use fusible hem tape or pins to hold in place, and edgestitch along both sides. Continue with Steps 5–8 and 12–13 to finish the key fob.

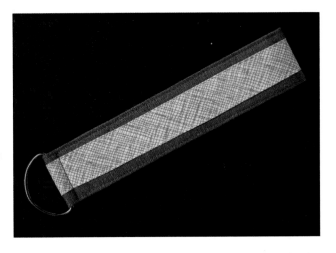

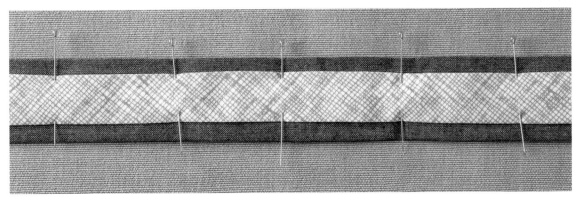

ALEXANDRA LEDGERWOOD is a modern quilt maker and designer from Overland Park, Kansas. She enjoys working improvisationally much of the time, creating one-of-a-kind quilts and quilted items for the home. Her quilt patterns have been featured in publications such as Modern Quilts Unlimited and Stitch Magazine. Alex is the author of *Improvising Tradition*. You can see more of her work on her blog, Teaginny Designs, teaginnydesigns. blogspot.com.

ZIPPER POUCH

A staple in any sewist's repertoire, this zipper pouch is sure to be in steady use around your home. Use it for makeup, a child's pencil pouch, or a handmade holder for your sewing notions. This pouch is also perfect for gifting, which is great once you discover how addictive these are to make! We've included tips for getting perfect points at your zipper ends, giving your finished product the look of a pro sewist. When you have this size mastered, get creative and craft pouches of different dimensions using longer zippers. Options for boxed corners and appliqué (page 101) mean you can really customize this for so many uses!

Features: Easy zipper, fully lined, sturdy interfacing, topstitching

Finished size: 6″ x 9″

Fabric: Choose home decor or quilting cotton for exterior and quilting cotton for interior.

GATHER
¼ yard OR 1 fat quarter for exterior

¼ yard OR 1 fat quarter for lining

½ yard fusible interfacing (such as Pellon SF101 Shape-Flex or fusible fleece)

9″ all-purpose polyester zipper

Zipper presser foot

Fabric marking pen

When you feel confident in the construction of this project, consider experimenting with different types of interfacing, such as Craft-Fuse. You can also use multiple layers of Shape-Flex woven interfacing for a stiffer exterior. The finished samples here are made with two layers of Shape-Flex.

CUT
(2) 10″ x 7″ from exterior fabric

(2) 10″ x 7″ from lining fabric

(2) 9″ x 6″ from interfacing (can double to give extra firmness to exterior)

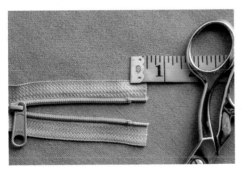

PREPARE

1. Center interfacing on wrong side of exterior fabric, glue side facedown. Iron according to manufacturer's instructions and following Interfacing 101 tips (see page 50). If adding double layer of interfacing, fuse them separately one right after the other.

2. Trim zipper tape ½″ beyond zipper stops on both ends so that zipper and tape together are 10″ long.

3. If adding an optional appliqué letter or shape, attach to lower left corner of one exterior fabric, 1¼″ to 2″ from bottom and one side. (See Extra Credit and Appliqué 101, page 101.)

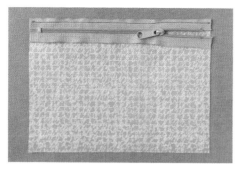

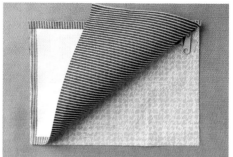

SEW

4. Place zipper and one lining piece right side up, aligning raw edges. Using zipper foot (with needle aligned to left side), baste along top ⅛" from top edge to hold zipper in place.

5. Place exterior fabric right side down and align with raw edges of zipper and lining. Pin through all three layers. Layers will be (from bottom to top): lining faceup, zipper faceup, exterior fabric facedown. Sew a seam close to zipper teeth, allowing presser foot to follow zipper teeth and backstitching at each end.

6. Open both fabrics away from zipper, positioning wrong sides together. Press. Take care with this step or zipper pull will catch on fabric.

7. Topstitch through all layers, close to previous seam.

ZIPPER SEWING 101

Sewing near a zipper pull can be tricky. Here's how to get a perfectly stitched zipper: As you sew and approach the zipper pull, stop just before the pull gets in the way. Lower the needle into the fabric and raise the presser foot. Move the zipper pull to a position behind the needle, which may mean reaching underneath layers of your project. Lower the presser foot and continue sewing.

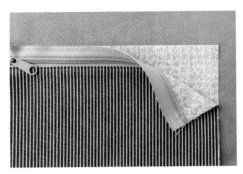

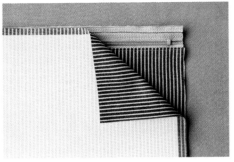

8. Position finished unit from Step 7 on top of remaining lining piece, top edges aligned. Lining fabrics will face each other, right sides together. Baste zipper unit to second lining piece, as in Step 4, to keep pieces neatly layered.

9. Place second exterior piece right side down on top of unit, aligning with top of zipper tape. Layer from bottom to top: lining faceup, finished unit from Step 7 zipper faceup, exterior fabric facedown. Sew a seam close to zipper teeth, allowing presser foot to follow zipper.

10. Repeat Steps 6 and 7.

11. Open zipper halfway.

12. Match lining to lining and exterior to exterior, right sides together, and pin. Finger press zipper tape at side seam toward lining fabric and pin down. This is important for a professional and finished look.

If adding box corners, cut 1″ or 1½″ squares from the two bottom corners of all four pieces of fabric before proceeding to Step 13. A 1″ corner will yield a pouch with a 1″-deep base, while a 1½″ cutout forms a 2″-deep base.

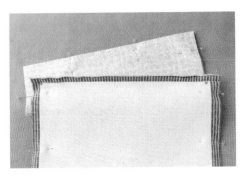

13. Feel along wrong side of fabric near zipper ends and mark zipper stops with fabric marking pen. This helps you keep your needle away from the stops. Mark a 2″ to 3″ opening along bottom of lining for turning.

▶ **TIP**
Double pin here in Step 13 so you remember to stop sewing when you reach each of the double pins.

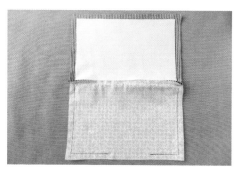

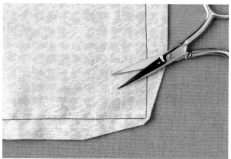

14. Sew around entire piece, using ½" seam and backstitching at each end. Take care to sew neatly and slowly at zipper. If omitting boxed corners, pivot at each corner, leaving needle in down position. For boxed corners, leave cutouts unsewn for now.

15. For pouch without boxed corners, clip and taper all four corners, being careful not to clip stitches, and proceed to Step 17.

16. For boxed corner pouch, pull open corner cutouts so that side and bottom seams meet and nest (meaning they go in opposite directions). Flatten unit to sew the corner, backstitching at each end. Repeat with remaining three corners.

17. Cut a notch in exterior and lining near both zipper ends. This reduces bulk and allows zipper ends to point nicely when turned right side out.

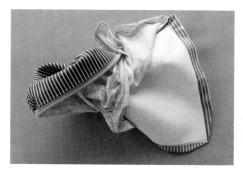

18. Turn right side out by pulling pouch through opening in lining. Push corners out using a turning tool. Tuck seam allowance in at lining opening and stitch closed close to edge of fold. Stuff lining fabric inside pouch.

19. For easier opening, and additional flair, tie a small length of thin grosgrain ribbon through the zipper tab.

EXTRA CREDIT

Appliqué a letter or shape to the outside of your pouch.

APPLIQUÉ 101

Raw edge fusible appliqué is a relatively easy skill for a beginner. Monograms or shapes add a personal touch to any project with a few basic steps. Needle-turn appliqué uses a needle and thread to tuck the raw edge of fabric under the shape. Here, appliqué is done by machine, finishing the raw edges by using a zigzag stitch to permanently secure the design to your project.

SUPPLIES NEEDED

Paper-backed fusible web, sewable variety (sold under the name WonderUnder and HeatnBond)

Project fabrics (minimum of 2)

Shape or letter to trace

Thread to match shape

Pencil

Paper scissors

Iron

1. Trace shape onto paper side of fusible web using pencil. If shape is not symmetrical, like most letters, be sure to trace the reverse image.

2. Cut out shape approximately ¼" outside of pencil line.

3. Fuse to wrong side of appliqué fabric, following manufacturer's instructions. Paper side will be face up.

4. Let cool, then cut out design along pencil line.

5. Peel off paper backing. Position on right side of project's fabric. Use iron to fuse in place. Allow to cool.

6. At your machine, attach an appliqué foot if you have one as this allows you to see your shape's edge as you sew. An all-purpose presser foot will work fine. Set machine to a zigzag stitch. I recommend a narrow width and a stitch length slightly closer together than default settings. Test stitches on scrap fabric until desired setting is found.

7. Beginning at a corner (if possible), sew around all raw edges of shape to secure appliqué to project's fabric. Aim to have outer point of zigzag stitch hit just beyond edge of appliqué shape. Backstitch once or lockstitch at end of stitches.

TIPS

▶ Invisible thread can be a nice option for appliqué. Some machines tolerate this better than others, so it test on scrap fabric first.

▶ Pivot with needle down at any curves or corners. Aim to have needle down at outermost point of zigzag when pivoting at corners, then rotate fabric and continue.

▶ Shapes may be layered and overlapped, but each should be stitched down before fusing the next layer on top.

▶ When choosing fonts, choose straight edges over swirls and script. Size 150 to 200 point font is suggested. Rockwell Extra Bold font is shown in sample. Print in mirror image if possible, or trace in reverse using a light box or window.

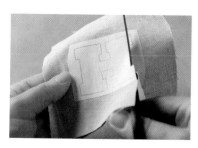

ZIP IT PILLOW

This throw pillow features a coordinating binding and a zipper hidden beneath a flap of fabric on the pillow back. It is truly a professional look! These pillows are a great place to show off a large-scale print. Hand binding is secretly my favorite step in making a quilt or pillow — it is portable and I can work on it while watching a favorite movie or visiting with my family. The School of Sewing ladies loved this step, and we hope you do, too!

Features: Binding, covered zipper, soft interfacing, removable, and washable cover

Finished size: 18″ x 18″

Fabric: Choose home decor or quilting cotton for main pillow and quilting cotton for binding. Small-scale prints, stripes, and plaids work well as binding choices.

GATHER
¾ yard for pillow

⅛ yard for binding

½ yard fusible fleece or fusible Thermolam interfacing

22″ all-purpose polyester zipper

18″ square pillow form

Hand-sewing needle

Clover Wonder Clips OR standard hair barrettes

Zipper presser foot

Fabric marking pen

CUT
18″ square for pillow front

18″ x 6″ and 18″ x 14″ for pillow back

18″ square fusible fleece interfacing

(2) 2¼″ x width of fabric binding strips

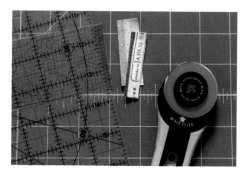

PREPARE
1. Center fusible fleece on wrong side of pillow front, fusible side down. Iron to fabric, following manufacturer's instructions.

See Extra Credit (page 109): If adding machine quilting to your pillow front, do so now.

2. Trim selvage edges from binding strips.

SEW

3. Place two binding strip ends, right sides together, at a 90-degree angle. Pin. Draw 45-angle line. Sew on line.

4. Trim seam allowance to ¼". Press seam open. Trim dog ears.

5. Press binding in half along length of strip, wrong sides together. Set aside.

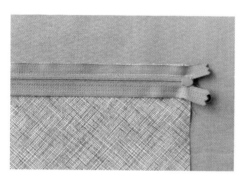

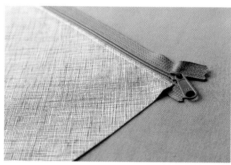

6. Place 18" x 14" backing fabric right side up. Center zipper facedown along one long edge. Sew together, using zipper presser foot.

7. Press fabric away from zipper and topstitch.

8. Press one long edge of remaining backing piece 1" to the wrong side of fabric. If using directional fabric, press along bottom of print.

9. Open pressed fold. Place this edge along zipper edge. Fabrics will be right sides together. Sew fabric to zipper.

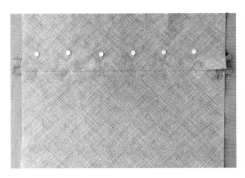

10. Refold fabric and press again if necessary. Flap will cover zipper. Backing unit should now measure 18" square. Adjust fold and press as needed to match this measurement. Pin flap to keep it from slipping.

11. Topstitch along upper edge of zipper flap, allowing zipper foot to follow zipper teeth.

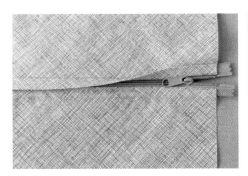

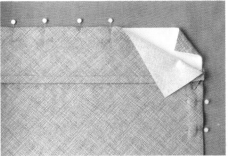

12. Place pillow back and pillow front wrong sides together on work surface. Move zipper pull so it is within edges of pillow. Trim zipper tape even with pillow edges. Pin around all four sides.

13. Using all-purpose presser foot, sew all sides with seam allowance just less than ¼", pivoting with needle down at each corner. Do not clip corners.

14. Finish pillow by following Binding 101 instructions (page 106).

BINDING 101

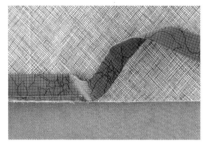

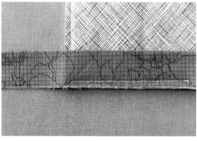

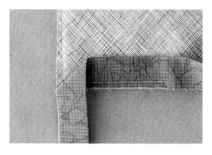

1. Place binding along bottom edge of pillow front, aligning raw edges of project and binding. Leaving 10″ of binding unsewn, sew using ¼″ seam allowance.

2. Stop sewing ¼″ from each corner. With needle down, pivot 45-degrees and sew off corner of the project. Cut threads and remove project from machine.

3. Rotate project to next edge. Flip up binding, forming 45-degree angle fold at corner.

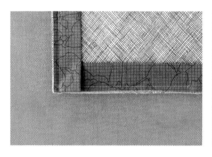

4. Fold binding back down along next edge. Be sure fold is even with top edge. There will be a flap of fabric at the corner. Pin flap down, if desired. Continue sewing along next side, starting at top edge. Repeat Steps 2–4 at remaining corners.

5. Stop sewing 8″ to 10″ from binding starting point. Backstitch. Trim one binding tail to end at center of gap.

6. Now you have two options for joining the tails: The Easy Way and My Favorite Way.

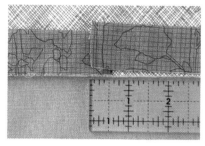
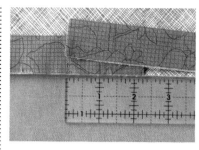
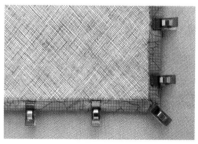

The Easy Way

Trim remaining binding tail so that binding pieces overlap by ½″. Trim perpendicular to binding. Open binding tails to match 2¼″ ends right sides together. Pin. Ensure tails are not twisted. Sew together using ¼″ seam allowance and finger press seam open.

My Favorite Way

Trim remaining binding tail so that binding pieces overlap by 2¼″. Open binding tails as illustrated, matching right sides together at a 90-degree angle. Pin. Mark 45-degree angle line. Check to be sure binding is not twisted. Sew along marked line. Trim seam allowance to ¼″ and finger press seam open.

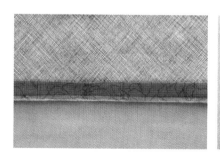

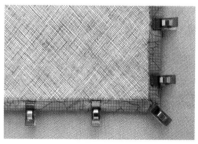

7. Refold binding along the length. Sew binding across gap, backstitching at each end.

8. Press binding away from project front on all four sides.

9. Fold binding around to back side of project. Use clips to hold in place. Clover Wonder Clips work well, as do standard hair barrettes.

LET'S LEARN THE LADDER STITCH!

It's a beautiful way to finish your binding by hand.

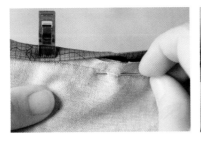

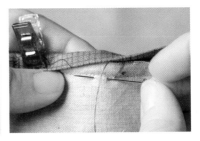

1. Thread needle, tying thread tails together in a knot at end to form a doubled thread for stitching. Beginning at center of one side, sew a stitch into project back at the outer edge, within the seam allowance. This hides your knot.

2. Insert needle into the backing and exit just outside the machine-stitched line where binding was sewn to the project. Next, insert needle into the fold of the binding directly above your stitch. Push needle along ¼" inside the fold and exit at fold.

3. Insert needle just outside machine-stitched line on project backing. Push needle along ¼" inside backing fabric. Take care to avoid the needle going through to project front. Exit just outside machine-stitched line. Notice how needle is primarily positioned parallel to fabric rather than being inserted straight into and out of fabric.

4. It is extremely important that these stitches are perpendicular from backing to binding. When you pull the thread, only a tiny dot of thread will show in the finished binding.

5. At corners, pull up needle where machine stitches intersect. Fold binding to miter the corner. This may take a few tries until you are happy with the appearance. Take one (tacking) stitch at inner edge. Repeat two more times. Push needle back down to restart the ladder stitch along next side of project.

6. When you reach the place you started, take an extra stitch and form a loop with the thread. Insert the needle through the loop and pull tight, forming a knot. Bury final stitches within edge of backing to keep them hidden.

> ▶ **TROUBLESHOOTING**
> **Your goal is for the stitches to be tight, but not so tight that you break the thread! Should the thread break, carefully pull out enough stitches to re-thread the broken ends onto your needle. Bury the ends within the seam allowance of the backing and begin a new length of thread.**

EXTRA CREDIT

To add extra dimension to your pillow, consider machine quilting the pillow top. After fusing fleece to the pillow front, quilt just as you would if following Steps 4–8 of the Set the Table Place Mats project (page 138). You won't have a backing and the fleece will act as a batting, but the process is essentially the same. An alternative is to form a "quilt sandwich" by layering the pillow front with batting and a muslin backing (which won't show on the final pillow). When you are finished quilting, trim the excess backing and batting to 18″ square, then proceed with the Zip It Pillow Step 2 (page 103).

CARRY-ALL CLUTCH

It's time for some fancy moves: sewing curves! Perfectly sized to hold a cell phone and other small essentials, with a zipper to keep items safely inside, this clutch is both useful and stylish. Tips for sewing curves make this project beginner-friendly. And the bonus? Using some simple hardware, you can attach your Ruffled Wristlet Key Fob from page 90!

Features: Sewn curves, hook and loop tape, zipper closure, sturdy interfacing, attached key fob

Finished size: 5″ x 8″

Fabric: Choose quilting cotton or home decor for exterior and quilting cotton for lining.

GATHER
¼ yard OR 1 fat quarter for exterior

¼ yard OR 1 fat quarter for lining

¼ yard fusible fleece (referred to as fleece in instructions)

½ yard Pellon 808 Craft-Fuse interfacing (referred to as interfacing in instructions)

4″ of ¾″-wide sew-in hook and loop tape

1″ D-ring OR 1″ swivel latch

9″ all-purpose polyester zipper

Zipper presser foot

Fabric marking pen

Templates A and B on page 153-154.

CUT
(2) 10″ x 6″ each from exterior fabric, lining fabric, fleece, and interfacing (total of eight pieces)

9″ x 5″ each from exterior fabric, lining fabric, fleece, and interfacing (total of four pieces)

2½″ x 3″ from exterior fabric for zipper tabs

2″ square from exterior fabric for loop

Use ¼″ seam allowance unless otherwise noted.

1. Iron fleece to wrong sides of all exterior pieces. Iron interfacing to wrong sides of all lining pieces.

2. Trace and cut Template A (main body) from all four 10″ x 6″ rectangles. Trace and cut Template B (flap) from both 9″ x 5″ rectangles. Rotary cut straight edges and use scissors on curves.

3. Trim Template A and B on solid line. Center on wrong side of corresponding pieces from Step 2. Trace around each piece. These marks will be your stitching lines and will help as you sew around the curves.

4. Position soft half of hook and loop tape strip on right side of flap lining. Hook and loop tape will be centered along length, 2″ from top edge of flap. Set remaining piece of hook and loop tape aside for now.

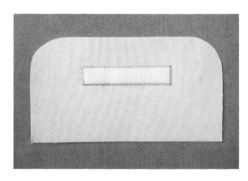

5. Sew around edge of hook and loop tape using zigzag stitch.

6. Cut zipper to exactly 8″. If you trim off the zipper stop, be sure you do not open the zipper all the way!

"I've received so many compliments on how cute the clutch is. And it wasn't as hard as I thought it would be!"
—CALI

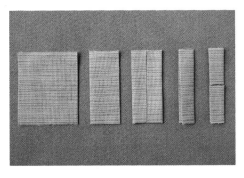

7. Press 2½″ x 3″ exterior fabric in half along 3″ side to form a 1¼″ x 3″ folded piece. Open and press raw edges to meet crease. Press in half lengthwise again. Cut in half, creating two 1½″ pieces.

8. Place end of zipper inside fold of fabric. Fold fabric down and over zipper end.

9. Topstitch close to inner edge of fabric. Trim fabric to match width of zipper. Repeat at opposite end of zipper, opening zipper pull to allow room for presser foot to sew. Be sure zipper tape ends are side by side: no gap and no overlap.

10. Pin flap pieces right sides together. Beginning at top right corner of flap, sew around the curved sides and bottom using a ½″ seam. Leave the straight edge un-sewn.

▶ **TIP**
Now that you know how to make zipper tape ends, you can use them to step up your game with the Zipper Pouches we made back on page 96! Just remember to cut your pouch 1″ wider than your prepared zipper.

CURVES 101

When sewing curves, follow the marked lines traced onto curve of project. Shorten stitch length to sew curve more easily. Pivot slightly as needed: rotate fabric with machine needle down and presser foot raised. Snip into seam for inner (concave) curves and cut V-shaped notches for outer (convex) curves. Be careful not to clip stitches!

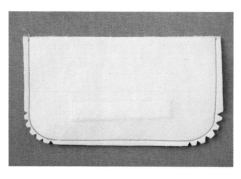

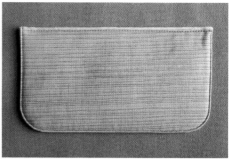

11. Trim seam allowance to ¼" and clip notches into curve. Use tip of scissors, being careful not to clip stitches.

12. Turn flap right side out. Carefully work to reshape the curve, using fingers or blunt turning tool. Press. Topstitch slowly around curved edge of flap, ⅛" from edge. Baste straight edge closed, sewing ⅛" from raw edges. Set flap aside.

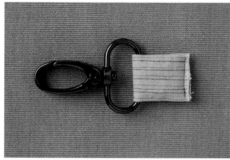

13. Fold 2" square in half, right sides together. Sew ¼" seam along long raw edge. Press seam open. Turn right side out, using safety pin to turn if necessary.

14. Press with seam centered on bottom. Fold and press loop in half. Slip D-ring or swivel clasp onto loop. Baste raw edges together.

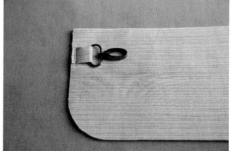

Attaching a swivel clasp in place of the D-ring will allow you to connect the ring of your key fob (page 91)!

15. Pin loop to left side of exterior front (with loop), raw edges together and 1" from top edge. Baste in place with ⅛" seam.

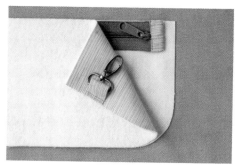

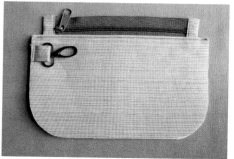

► **TIP**

As you near the zipper pull, stop with needle down. Raise presser foot and move zipper pull behind needle. Lower presser foot and continue sewing.

16. Place zipped zipper and one lining piece right side up, with zipper pull on the right. Align raw edges, keeping the zipper centered on the lining. Baste in place, if desired, to keep from shifting. Place exterior front fabric (with loop) right side down and align with raw edges of zipper and lining. Pin through all three layers. Layers will be: lining fabric faceup, zipper faceup, exterior fabric facedown.

17. Using zipper presser foot (needle on left side), sew ¼″ seam close to zipper teeth, backstitching at each end.

18. Place wrong side of fabrics together. Press fabric away from zipper tape. Take care with this step or zipper pull will catch on fabric. Topstitch through all layers, close to previous seam.

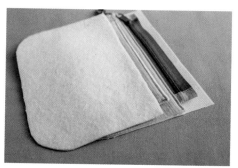

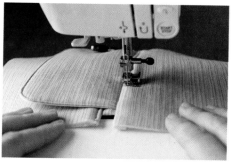

19. Position flap and remaining pieces as shown, top edges aligned. Layers will be: lining faceup, finished unit from Step 18 zipper faceup, completed flap exterior faceup, exterior fabric facedown. Ensure all layers are centered. Layers are separated here for illustration purposes. Sew close to zipper teeth, as in Step 17.

20. Position wrong side of front pieces together. Position wrong side of back pieces together. Press fabric away from zipper tape. Topstitch through all back piece layers, close to previous seam. Ensure that flap is exterior side up so it stays out of the way.

► **TIP**
This is thick and will be tricky. Sew slowly. Use Wonder Clips instead of pins.

21. Switch to all-purpose presser foot. Place remaining hook and loop tape piece in position to match up with closed flap. Find the accurate placement by holding the clutch as if it were finished. Pin hook and loop tape in place through exterior front only.

22. Sew in place with zigzag stitch through exterior front. Do not sew through lining.

23. Open zipper entirely.

24. Match lining to lining and exterior to exterior, right sides together, and pin. Be sure loop is not sticking out and is tucked in between layers for sewing. Finger press zipper tape at side seam toward the lining fabric and pin down. This is important for a professional and finished look.

▶ **TIP**
Fabric thickness can make sewing at Step 26 tricky! Use a denim needle for extra strength, if desired. Sew slowly and use your machine's handwheel at the zipper tape to sew one stitch at a time if necessary.

25. Mark a 4″ to 5″ opening along bottom of lining for turning. Double pin here so you remember to stop sewing.

26. Starting at opening at bottom of lining, sew around entire piece, using ½″ seam allowance. Sew slowly at curved corners, pivoting slightly as needed. Take care to sew neatly and slowly near zipper. Seam should be right next to but not over zipper tape. Sew back and forth over loop seam two times to reinforce.

27. Trim seam allowance to ¼″ and clip curves of corners. Cut notch at zipper tape to remove excess bulk. Turn right side out, pulling through opening left in lining.

28. Tuck in seam allowance at opening and stitch closed near edge of fold. Stuff lining fabric inside clutch.

29. For easier opening, and additional flair, tie a small length of thin grosgrain ribbon through the zipper tab.

EXTRA CREDIT

Make a larger 8″ x 12″ clutch for carrying more. Enlarge Templates A and B by 150% using your computer and printer or at a copy center. Note that seam allowances will also be enlarged, so you'll want to mark your own dashed-line ½″ seam allowance outside of the solid lines on the enlarged templates.

Increase fabrics to ½ yard each, interfacing to 1 yard, hook and loop tape to 6″ length, and use a 14″ zipper. Change cutting instructions to: (2) 14″x 19″ rectangles each from exterior fabric, lining fabric, fleece, and interfacing (total of eight pieces), and a 14″ x 8″ rectangle each from exterior fabric, lining fabric, fleece, and interfacing (total of four pieces).

Center hook and loop tape and sew 4″ from top edge of flap at Step 4. Trim the 14″ zipper to 12″ at Step 7. Follow all patterns steps as directed for regular clutch.

TECH CASE

Skip the store-bought covers and give your tablet a stylish, padded, and functional home. The Tech Case is custom-fit for any device, with or without its cover. Design your case with a pocket perfectly sized to fit your phone, earbuds, or charging cords. Our class loved the ability to customize, but they were most impressed with how quickly they learned to sew a buttonhole. You'll be amazed at how easy a buttonhole really is to sew! Alternatively, use a hook and loop tape closure in lieu of a button by following the instructions in the Extra Credit.

Features: Sew a curve, sew a buttonhole, sew a button, custom pocket, protective padding

Finished size: varies by device

Fabric: Choose home decor or quilting cotton for exterior and quilting cottons for remaining pieces.

GATHER
⅓ yard OR 1 fat quarter exterior fabric

⅓ yard OR 1 fat quarter lining fabric

¼ yard OR 1 fat quarter accent fabric for flap

¼ yard OR 1 fat quarter fabric for pocket

½ yard fusible fleece, sometimes called quilter's fleece (referred to as fleece in instructions)

1 yard woven fusible interfacing, such as Pellon SF101 Shape-Flex (referred to as interfacing in instructions)

⅝"–1" button

Buttonhole foot

Fabric marking pen

Hand-sewing needle

Flap Template on page 155

Ditch or edgestitch foot (optional)

MEASURE
Measure and record the dimensions of your device, including the cover if you wish to use it along with this fabric case. Round up to the nearest quarter inch and always double check your measurements.

Width: _____

Height: _____

Depth: _____

A = width + depth + 1":
My Measurement A is _____"

B = height + depth + 1":
My Measurement B is _____"

C = width + depth:
My Measurement C is _____"

D = height + depth:
My Measurement D is _____"

CUT
Fill in the cutting list below with your measurements. Note: Fleece dimensions will be one inch smaller in length and width than fabric pieces.

From exterior fabric
(2) _____ A x _____ B

From lining fabric
(2) _____ A x _____ B

(1) flap (use template)

From pocket fabric
(1) _____ A x _____ B

From accent fabric
(1) flap (use template)

From interfacing
(3) _____ C x _____ D

(1) flap (use template)

From fleece
(4) _____ C x _____ D

(1) flap (use template)

1. Center fleece on wrong sides of both exterior pieces. Fuse. Repeat, to create double layer of fleece on each exterior piece. Center and fuse interfacing to wrong sides of both lining pieces and pocket. Fuse fleece to wrong sides of flap exterior. Fuse interfacing to wrong sides of flap lining.

2. Pin flap pieces right sides together. Beginning at top right corner of flap, sew around curved side using ½" seam. Leave straight edge un-sewn. Backstitch at each end.

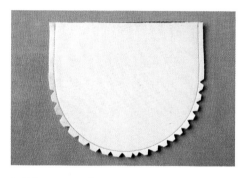

3. Trim seam allowance to ¼" and clip notches into seam allowance at curve, taking care not to clip stitches. Turn flap right side out. Press. Topstitch along curve. An edgestitch foot is helpful for topstitching.

STOP! It's buttonhole time! Sew buttonhole into flap, following Buttonholes 101 instructions (opposite). Start buttonhole at point marked on template piece.

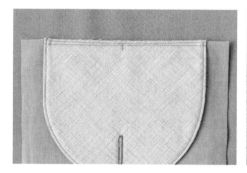

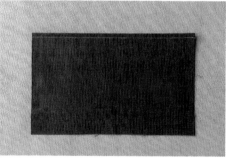

5. Once buttonhole is finished, change back to all-purpose presser foot. Find and mark center of flap and top of one exterior piece. Pin flap to top, matching centers. Flap lining and right side of exterior will be faceup. Baste along top edge using ¼" seam allowance.

6. Fold pocket in half, wrong sides together. Press. Folded pocket should have same width as exterior front. Topstitch along folded edge of pocket, ¼" from fold.

BUTTONHOLES 101

Making a buttonhole is easier than you might think! First, grab your sewing machine manual. Each machine is different, and you'll want to refer to the instructions specific to your machine. Having said that, most work similarly to these steps:

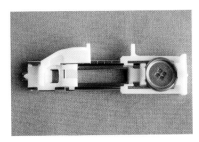

1. Insert button into buttonhole foot and push together tightly around button. This is how your machine knows how large to make the buttonhole.

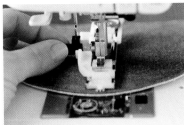

2. Attach buttonhole foot to machine and select buttonhole stitch. Lower buttonhole lever down as far as it will go. Don't forget this! Lowering the lever is the one step people forget most!

3. Always make a test buttonhole using fabric scraps that are the same fabric type and thickness as the fabric in your project. In our case, you'll want to put some exterior fabric, lining fabric, fleece, and interfacing together, just like the layers in your actual project. There's no need to make the full flap again. A piece roughly 3″ square is plenty.

4. Place test fabric under foot and lower the foot. Following instructions in manual, begin making buttonhole by pressing foot pedal. Notice how the machine sews backward to the rear of the buttonhole first. The buttonhole will be automatically sewn and the machine should stop on its own. Raise presser foot and snip threads.

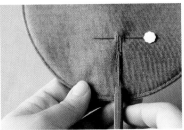

5. Place a pin perpendicular to the end of the buttonhole. This will stop your seam ripper from going too far. Using seam ripper, open center of buttonhole. Test button to be sure it will fit through opening.

6. Mark desired location for buttonhole on project using fabric marking pen. Once you are satisfied with the test buttonhole, position your project under buttonhole foot with end of placement marking directly under needle. Remember, the buttonhole will be sewn *behind* that mark. Repeat buttonhole steps above to create buttonhole in project.

"I found that it was helpful to do a buttonhole test on a scrap piece of fabric layers before putting it on the flap of my case. That gave me a chance to make corrections and I was so glad that I didn't mess it up on the real thing!"

—AMY

7. Pin pocket to right side of remaining exterior piece, aligning raw edges on sides and bottom. Baste in place along sides and bottom with ¼″ seam allowance. Pivot at corners with needle down.

8. Place exterior pieces right sides together. Pocket and flap will be at opposite ends. Pin and sew along both long sides and bottom, using ½″ seam. Top edge will be left open. Clip and taper corners and press seams open.

9. Place lining pieces right sides together. Mark a 4″ opening along bottom edge. Pin and sew along both sides and bottom, using ½″ seam. Press seams open, including opening in bottom edge, and clip corners.

10. Turn exterior right side out. Place exterior inside lining, right sides together. Match side seams and pin around top edge. Be sure flap is tucked down into project and is between lining and exterior.

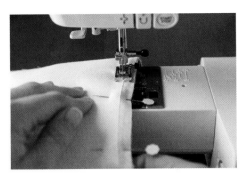

11. Sew around top edge of project with ½″ seam allowance, using free arm feature of sewing machine. Sew slowly over flap area, as this area will be thick.

12. Pull cover right side out through opening in lining. Tuck seam allowance in at opening and edgestitch closed. Stuff lining inside exterior. Press around opening, rolling seam using fingers to wiggle seam allowance flat.

13. Topstitch around opening, using ¼″ seam allowance and starting at side seam. Using extra care here will yield a professional finish, so take your time. You will not be topstitching on the flap for this step.

14. Insert device into cover and lower the flap. Mark button placement through buttonhole with fabric marker. Remove device and hand sew button to exterior front, using double thickness of thread.

EXTRA CREDIT

Change up the design by using hook and loop tape in place of the buttonhole. Purchase 3″ of ¾″- wide sew-in hook and loop tape. After Step 1, sew soft piece to the flap lining, 3½″ from top raw edge. At Step 6, sew the hook piece to the exterior front, 2½″ from top raw edge. The hook and loop tape is sewn around all four edges of the piece using a straight stitch or zigzag, backstitching or lockstitching at start and stop.

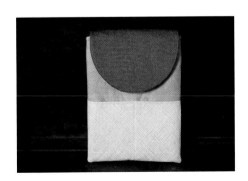

ESSENTIAL TOTE BAG

Hands down, this project was the class favorite. I've lost track of how many tote bags the School of Sewing students have made! It's perfectly sized for an overnight or to carry a giant stack of library books. You can even use it as a grocery bag! Choose between a solid or striped exterior, short or long handles. An added bonus? It can be reversible, with your optional interior pocket suddenly becoming an accent on the exterior!

CUT
Striped Style (page 129)
4 exterior stripes A-D (top to bottom):

A, B, C = (2) 4½" x 21" each

D (bottom stripe) = (2) 7" x 21"

Solid Style (shown at left)
(2) 21"W x 17½"L from exterior fabric

Both Styles
(2) 21"W x 17½"L from lining fabric

(2) 21" x 17½" interfacing

(2) 20" x 16½" Thermolam

(2) 6" x 31½" each of strap fabric and interfacing for long straps OR (2) 6" x 20" each of strap fabric and interfacing for short straps

Optional pocket: (1) 9" x 11" each of any fabric and of interfacing

Sew with ½" seam allowance, unless otherwise noted.

1. Fuse interfacing to wrong side of straps and lining. If making short straps, fuse interfacing to entire length of strap fabric. If making long straps, fuse interfacing strips end to end to cover length of entire strap. For solid bag, proceed to Step 2. For striped bag, see Sewing the Stripes sidebar.

2. Center and fuse Thermolam to wrong side of both exteriors.

3. Cut 3" square from two bottom corners of each lining and exterior panel. Set panels aside.

4. Fold strap piece in half along length and press. Open fold and bring long sides to center fold. Press. Press in half along length again, encasing raw edges.

Features:
Topstitching, boxed corners, interior pocket, strap length options, pieced stripes

Finished size: 19" x 15"

Fabric: Choose quilting cotton or home decor fabric for exterior and quilting cotton for lining.

GATHER
Striped Style
¼ yard of four different fabrics for exterior

Solid Style
⅔ yard for exterior

Both Styles
⅔ yard for lining

½ yard for long straps OR ¼ yard for short straps

2 yards woven fusible interfacing, such as Pellon SF101 (referred to as interfacing in instructions)

⅔ yard Pellon fusible 971F Thermolam Plus interfacing (referred to as Thermolam in instructions)

Optional pocket: 9" x 11" (half a fat quarter) each of pocket fabric and of interfacing

Fabric marking pen

Hand-sewing needle

Ditch or edgestitch foot (optional)

For added stiffness, separately fuse two layers of woven interfacing to exterior panels, followed by one layer of Thermolam. An additional 2½ yards of interfacing are needed for this modification.

5. Topstitch strap ⅛″ and ¼″ from both sides. Trim threads at end of strap. If your machine has trouble grabbing the edge of the strap to start, use a fabric leader (page 58).

6. Repeat Steps 3 through 5 with remaining strap.

Add optional interior pocket(s) here if desired. See Simple Pockets 101 (below) and Extra Credit (page 128).

SIMPLE POCKETS 101: SEWING AN INTERIOR POCKET

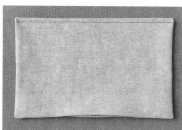

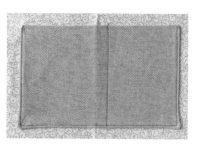

1. Fuse interfacing to wrong side of pocket fabric. Fold and press pocket unit in half along shortest side, right sides together. Pocket will measure 9″ x 5½″.

2. Sew along both sides and bottom using ¼″ seam allowance, leaving 4″ opening along bottom edge for turning. Clip and taper all corners.

3. Turn pocket right side out. Use a chopstick or point turner to push out points. Press. Tuck in seam allowance at opening in bottom edge.

4. Topstitch across top of pocket (the folded edge, not the edge with the opening) using ¼″ seam.

5. Fold pocket and one lining piece in half to find centers. Pin pocket on right side of lining, 4″ from top edge with center marks aligned.

6. Edgestitch pocket along both sides and bottom, catching and closing the bottom opening with stitches. Reinforce with extra stitches at top of both sides.

7. You now have a lovely interior pocket. Resume tote sewing directions at Step 7.

Optional: Place frequently used items, such as a cell phone or pen, in the pocket and mark a customized stitching line to divide pocket. Sew from top to bottom to divide pocket into desired sections.

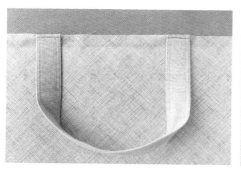

7. Pin straps to top edge of exterior panels 5½″ from each side edge, right sides together and raw edges aligned. Ensure strap is not twisted. Sew in place with ¼″ seam.

8. Pin bottom edge of exterior pieces right sides together and sew. Press seam to one side.

9. Open unit flat and topstitch ¼″ from bottom seam in the same direction you pressed. (You'll sew through only one layer of the exterior and then both layers of the seam allowance underneath.)

10. Pin exterior pieces right sides together. Sew. Corner squares will remain unsewn. Press side seams open.

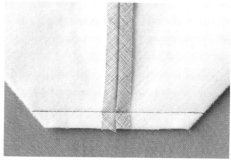

11. Pin lining pieces right sides together. Sew along both sides, leaving both corner cutouts unsewn. Sew bottom, leaving 6″ opening in center for turning. Press ½″ seam allowance open at opening to allow for a nice, easy finish at the end.

12. Open corner notches, pinching to bring side and bottom seams together. Pin. Sew, backstitching at each end and creating boxed corner. Repeat with all four corners: two lining and two exterior.

13. With exterior right side out and lining wrong side out, place exterior unit inside lining unit. Ensure straps are tucked inside between exterior and interior. Match side seams and pin or clip around entire top. Pin at side seams first, then centers of both panels and at straps, then one or two pins in between.

EXTRA CREDIT

Install a zippered pocket on one side of the lining and a regular pocket on the other! Follow the instructions in Zipper Pockets 101, page 134. Use the same size zipper and cutting dimensions as described in the Pleated Purse project. Install this zipper after Step 6 of tote instructions.

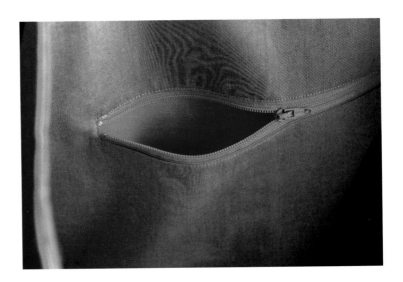

"It is definitely worth going slowly to make sure that the seams are straight, especially on the straps. They are a very visible part of the bag, and crooked seams would be noticeable."

—AMY

14. Sew around top of bag using free arm of sewing machine, starting at a side seam. Use extra stitching at straps to reinforce. I sew over each strap, then backstitch over the whole strap and then sew forward.

15. Pull bag through opening in lining. Tuck seam allowance in lining opening. Edgestitch closed.

16. Stuff lining in bag. Press top edge. Using care here results in a professional finish, so take your time!

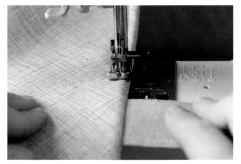

17. Topstitch ¼″ and ½″ around top of bag. Use free arm feature of sewing machine for this step and sew slowly. These stitches will show, so leave needle down to raise presser foot and adjust as often as necessary.

18. Tack lining to bag exterior at base, if desired. Using hand-sewing needle and double thickness of thread, sew in seam line at boxed corner. You'll want these stitches hidden, so take your time here. Use a thimble if pushing needle through thick interfacing proves difficult.

"I think this has been my favorite project so far. I was shocked at how easy it was to make this bag! I use it all the time."
—CHERYL

SEWING THE STRIPES

1. Arrange stripes in order, with 7″ wide piece on bottom. Pin and sew along long edges, using ½″ seam. Set seams and press open. Exterior unit should measure 21″ x 17½″. Repeat with remaining exterior stripes.

2. Center and fuse Thermolam to wrong side of each piece.

3. Topstitch ¼″ away from both sides of each seam for decorative finish or, if you're feeling adventurous, quilt the bag exterior every ¼″ as in the sample at right.

4. Resume tote sewing directions at Step 3.

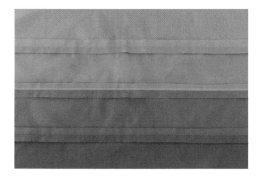

PLEATED PURSE

This sophisticated bag is large enough to carry the essentials but not so big that it becomes a bottomless pit. Stylish features such as refined pleats and a single strap make the Pleated Purse an excellent everyday purse. Sharpen your skills with the interior zippered pocket (it's really not hard!) and show off your topstitching ability on your very own custom purse. Extra interfacing gives the purse body without making the bag too stiff. Once you've mastered the basic pattern, make another, this time modifying the size and curve of the purse with the Extra Credit option for a stylish two-handled tote.

Features: Magnetic snaps, pleats, zippered interior pocket, boxed corners, topstitching

Finished size:

11″ x 13″ x 4″

Fabric: Choose quilting cotton or home decor fabric for exterior, and quilting cottons for lining and pockets.

GATHER
1½ yard exterior fabric

½ yard lining fabric

1 fat quarter or ¼ yard pocket fabric

3 yards woven fusible interfacing, such as Pellon SF101 Shape-Flex (referred to as interfacing in instructions)

(2) 1½″ x 1½″ fusible fleece scraps for snap reinforcement (referred to as fleece in instructions)

¾″ magnetic snap

9″ all-purpose polyester zipper

Zipper presser foot

Fabric marking pen

Ditch or edgestitching foot (optional)

Quarter-inch foot (optional)

CUT
From exterior
5″ x 26″ for strap

(2) 17″ x 3¾″ for upper purse body

(2) 20″ x 10¾″ for main purse body

From lining
(2) 17″ x 13½″

From pocket fabric
9″W x 11″L for simple pocket

(2) 11″ x 6″ for zipper pocket

From Interfacing
5″ x 26″ for strap

(4) 17″ x 3¾″ for upper purse body

(4) 20″ x 10¾″ for main purse body

(2) 17″ x 13½″ for lining

9″ x 11″ for simple pocket

SEW
Use ½″ seam allowance unless otherwise noted.

1. Iron interfacing to wrong sides of all exterior, lining, and simple pocket pieces, centering on each piece. Exterior upper and main body will have two layers of interfacing, each fused separately.

2. Fold strap piece in half along length, wrong sides together, and press. Open fold and bring long sides to center fold. Press. Press in half along length again, encasing raw edges

3. Topstitch ⅛'' from edge on both sides of strap. A ditch or edgestitching foot is useful here. Set strap aside.

4. Make a mark 1½'' from each corner along bottom edge of both main body pieces. Use ruler and rotary cutter to cut at angle from mark to top corner of main purse piece. Do not cut this angle on the lining pieces.

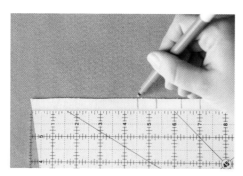

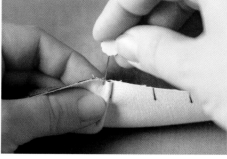

5. Mark pleats with fabric marking pen on top of wrong side of one main body piece. Beginning at top left corner, mark at 4½'', 5¼'', 6¼'', 7'', 13'', 13¾'', 14¾'', and 15½'' across top edge of piece. Repeat with remaining main body piece.

6. Match neighboring pleat marks, pinching wrong sides together at marks and forming a pleat. If seeing your marks is difficult, clip each one with a ⅛'' cut and match the cuts. Pin with right side of pleat pointing away from the center of the bag. Repeat with remaining three sets of pleat marks for a total of four pleats.

7. Examine purse from right side, ensuring that pleats are folded in correct direction: two on the left should point left and two on the right should point right. Stitch pleats in place using ¼'' seam. A quarter-inch foot is useful here.

8. Press top 2″ of pleats, allowing lower portion to fade into main body of bag. Top and bottom edges of main purse body should now measure 17″, though they may not appear to due to an upward curve caused by the pleats. Measure to be sure.

9. Pin and sew upper purse body to main purse body, right sides together. I find it helpful to sew with wrong side of pleats facing up. Press seam toward upper purse body.

10. Topstitch ¼″ from previous seam on upper purse body. Repeat Steps 7—10 with remaining exterior pieces.

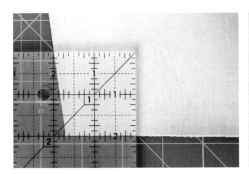

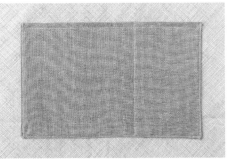

11. Cut a 2″ square from bottom corners of both exterior units and from both lining pieces. Because of the angled cut at lower corners of exterior, there will not be a 90-degree angle at the lower corner as you find and mark the 2″ square.

12. Add an interior zipper pocket like a pro. You can do this! Follow instructions in Zipper Pockets 101 (page 134).

Add interior pocket on remaining lining piece, if desired. Position the pocket 3½″ from top of lining. Follow directions from Simple Pockets 101, page 126.

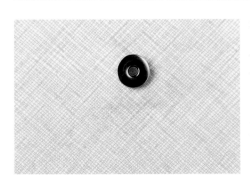

13. Fuse a 2″ square scrap of fleece or interfacing at snap location to reinforce wrong side of fabric. Locate and mark center top of each lining. Mark snap location at center top of bag lining, positioning top of snap 1½″ from top edge of lining. Install magnetic snaps, following manufacturer's instructions.

ZIPPER POCKETS 101

I promise it's not hard to install an interior zipper pocket. Just take your time and you'll have a fancy zipper pocket before you know it!

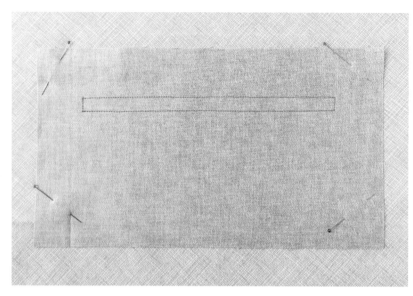

1. Mark the outline of the zipper sewing guide on wrong side of one zipper pocket piece. Use template found in the Templates section, page 153, or mark your own guide at ⅜″ x 8″. Position 1½″ from top edge and center along length.

2. Place zipper pocket piece on one lining piece, right sides together. Position pocket 2½″ from top edge of lining and center along width. Pin in three or four places outside zipper sewing guide marks.

3. Sew around entire guide on marked line. (It feels counterintuitive, but hang with me. Trust me: it will work!)

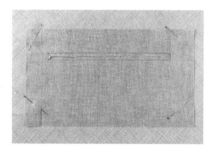

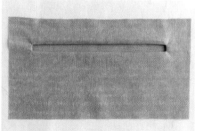

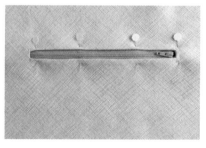

4. Cut down center of zipper guide, angling to cut into each corner without clipping stitches. You will cut through both the lining and the pocket fabric here.

5. Push all the pocket fabric through opening in lining. Press edges of opening flat. If puckers form at corners of opening, return to Step 4 and cut a bit farther into each corner.

6. Iron zipper flat if needed. Flip lining so right side is up. Position zipper under opening, ensuring that zipper pull is within opening. Pin in place or use fusible hem tape, if desired, for a more secure hold while sewing. I find it helpful to pin at ends first, then along the length. Reposition pins and zipper tape until you are satisfied with the placement.

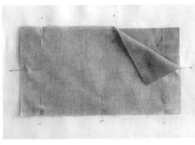

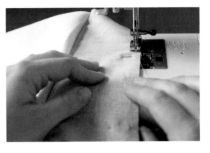

7. Change to zipper foot, with needle position on left. Sew around zipper, edgestitching with ⅛″ seam. Stop with needle down to raise presser foot to pivot and move zipper pull as needed. Be sure flaps of pocket fabric are not under the needle.

8. Flip lining so wrong side is up. Trim off excess zipper tape. Pin remaining pocket piece to pocket, right sides together. Pin only through both pocket fabrics. Do not pin into lining.

9. Change to all-purpose presser foot. Sew around entire pocket piece with ¼″ seam allowance, taking care to keep lining out of the way. I find it helpful to sew with lining right side up and the pocket on bottom. Keep the lining out of the way as you sew each side of the pocket.

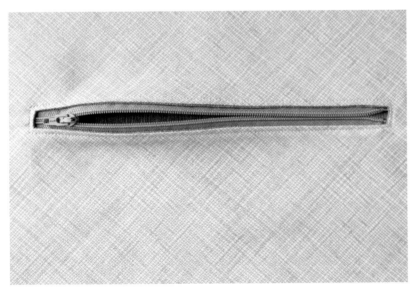

You did it! A real zipper pocket! Give yourself a high five! Now, return to Step 13 and finish your purse.

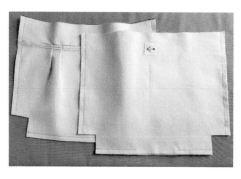

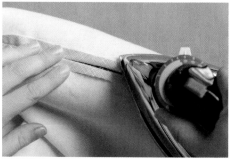

14. Pin main body pieces right sides together. Sew along both sides and across bottom, leaving top edge and both corner cutouts un-sewn. Repeat with lining pieces, this time leaving a 6″ opening along bottom for turning. Backstitch both sides of this opening.

15. Press open all exterior and lining side and bottom seams. Some spots are a tight fit, so use a seam roll or tightly rolled towel to press. Press seam allowance open at opening in lining. This will come in handy later.

16. Pull open corner cutouts so that side and bottom seams meet. Sew boxed corner, backstitching at each end. Repeat with remaining corners on exterior and lining.

17. Pin strap to exterior, centering at side seams with exterior fabrics together. Raw edges will be aligned. Ensure strap is not twisted. Baste in place with ¼″ seam.

18. Place exterior inside lining fabric, right sides together. Straps will be sandwiched between these layers. Match side seams and centers, pinning and sewing around entire opening, starting at a side seam.

"An important thing that I was reminded of was not to rush the last few steps. It's easy to get in the homestretch and get ahead of yourself. Once I got home I was trimming a few stray strings and admiring my work and then realized my simple pocket on the inside was upside down!"
—AMY

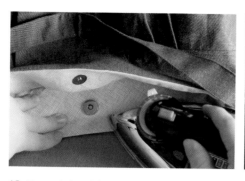 

19. Turn right side out, using hole in lining. Tuck in seam allowance at hole and edgestitch closed. Stuff lining into purse.

20. Press top of purse, using your fingers to wiggle top seam flat for a professional finish. Topstitch around entire top using ¼″ seam. A quarter-inch foot is useful here. Use your machine's free arm and take your time as these stitches will show. Stop with needle down to pivot as needed and keep strap out of the way. Sew slowly at centers to prevent magnetic snaps from running into the presser foot.

EXTRA CREDIT

Change up the look of the purse to make it more tote-like. Here's how: Increase the height of the main bag body and lining by 3″. Cut (2) 5″ x 22″ strips each from strap fabric and woven interfacing. Instead of cutting out boxed corners, mark and cut the angle in Step 4, then trace the curve of a CD or large glass onto both bottom corners of the lining and exterior. A 8½″ diameter salad plate was used in the sample. Sew together as in Step 15, ignoring corner instructions and instead clipping curved seam allowance. Leave an opening in lining for turning. Position straps along upper bag body, 5″ from each side edge, as you did in the Essential Tote Bag project on page 124. Try a contrasting fabric for the upper body and straps for a completely different look!

SET THE TABLE PLACE MATS

Dress up your table in a practical (and washable!) way as you learn machine quilting on this project. You'll make four reversible place mats, choosing two main fabrics and a coordinating binding. Use Insul-Bright heat-resistant batting and your project instantly becomes a trivet! Use this same idea in a smaller scale and you'll have the recipe for pot holders. The Extra Credit pieced option offers a beautiful way to make use of your fabric stash.

Features: Machine quilting, hand sewn binding, pin basting, batting

Finished size: 14″ x 20″

Fabric: Use only quilting cottons for this project.

GATHER
1 yard main fabric

1½ yards backing fabric

¾ yard binding fabric

1 yard batting OR crib-sized bag of batting

Painter's tape

Walking foot (preferred)

Curved safety pins (size 2 recommended)

Fabric marking pen (optional)

CUT
(4) 15″ x 21″ from main fabric

(4) 17″ x 23″ from backing fabric

(8) 2¼″ x width of fabric strips from binding fabric

(4) 16″ x 22″ from batting

1. Place backing right side down on work surface. Use painter's tape to secure backing edges to the work surface to keep fabric from moving.

2. Place batting on top of backing. Place main fabric on batting, right side up. Center all layers and smooth to eliminate wrinkles.

▶ **TIP**

If desired, use an erasable fabric marking pen to draw or trace a quilting design on the right side of the main fabric before you assemble the project layers.

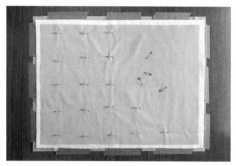

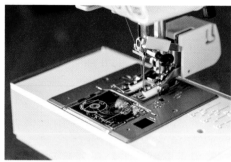

3. Pin layers (baste) with curved safety pins. The result is often called a "quilt sandwich." Begin pinning at center, pinning every 3″ to 4″, smoothing out as you work. Repeat with remaining pieces until you have four "quilt sandwiches."

4. Attach walking foot or all-purpose presser foot to sewing machine.

WALKING FOOT

A walking foot is especially useful for quilting or working with slippery or thick fabrics. When using the all-purpose foot, only the feed dogs move the fabric through the machine. A walking foot has grips on the actual foot, so the fabric is advanced through the machine evenly from top and bottom. This helps eliminate wrinkles and puckers in your quilting. Read the instructions that come with your particular walking foot for proper installation. If your walking foot comes with an adjustable guide bar, use it to make evenly spaced lines of quilting. Do this by setting the guide bar at a desired distance from the needle and running the guide bar along a previous stitching line.

"The walking foot = best sewing tool ever for a perfectionist! I loved it! Just follow that bar and it'll make my quilting lines perfectly spaced? I've so got this!"

—WHITNEY

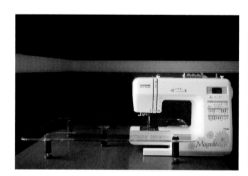

5. Attach an extension table to your machine if one is available. This supports your project and keeps your work surface nice and flat.

Painter's tape can be used to create a straight line path and is easily removed and repositioned. Use the tape as a guide for the edge of your presser foot. Just be sure you don't sew through the painter's tape!

6. Set stitch length slightly larger than regular sewing length, such as 2.4. It's a good idea to use a test "quilt sandwich" to try out a variety of stitch settings before you begin quilting your project.

7. Begin quilting in center portion of place mat, with stitches starting and ending in batting area. No need to backstitch here! Check back of project to ensure proper thread tension before continuing.

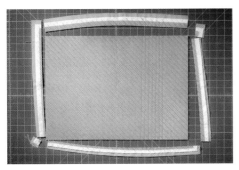

8. Continue quilting your way to the side edges, removing pins as you work. Don't forget to relax your shoulders. It's easy to tense up!

9. Trim quilted place mat to 14″ x 20″.

10. Trim selvages from binding strips. Sew binding strips into four sets of two strips each. Prepare each strip for binding and sew to quilt using instructions from Binding 101, page 106.

▶ **TIP**
Use a different thread color to accent quilting in one area of your project. Consider using the triple stitch, which is available on many machines as a decorative stitch, to add a thick line of quilting to your project.

EXTRA CREDIT

Sew a pieced place mat using (3) 1½″ x 15″ scraps of fabric and a ¼″ seam allowance. Press seams open for a flat finish. Background pieces will be 5½″ x 15″ and 13″ x 15″. Cut backing and binding as instructed above.

MY FIRST QUILT

Quilts are quite possibly my favorite thing to sew. I take that back. They are *positively* my favorite thing to sew. Sure, they take some time to complete, but you can't beat the impact they make, especially if they will be given to someone to celebrate or commemorate an important life event.

So here we are: the final exam of School of Sewing. Can you make a quilt? Of course you can! If you've made the Zip It Pillow and Set the Table Place Mats, you've already learned several of the skills needed. This quilt is made with one block, the half-square triangle. There are limitless designs and looks possible using one simple block. I dare you to make just one quilt!

Features: Matching seams, pieced half-square triangles, machine quilting, hand-sewn binding

Finished size: 40" x 48" baby quilt OR 60" x 72" lap quilt

Fabric: Use only quilting cottons for this project. Small-scale prints, solids, and near solids work best. Avoid large-scale prints. The more fabrics used, the greater the depth and variety in your quilt.

GATHER
Clear acrylic ruler

Fabric marker or Chaco liner (page 156)

Painter's tape

Curved safety pins for basting (size 2 recommended)

Quarter-inch presser foot (recommended)

Walking foot (recommended)

Extension table (recommended)

Fabric marking pen (optional)

GATHER CONT.
First, decide on a size and whether you want to make a quilt with two fabrics or many different fabrics. Several choices are shown in the Quilt Layout Options graphic (page 150). Once you've decided, stick to the fabric amounts — and later the cutting instructions — for that column only.

MATERIAL	BABY *(two color)*	BABY *(multicolor)*	LAP *(two color)*	LAP *(multicolor)*
Fabric A and B	1¼ yards each	—	2½ yards each	—
Background Fabric	—	1¼ yards	—	2½ yards
Accent Fabrics	—	(8) ¼ yard	—	(10) ¼ yard
Backing	3 yards	3 yards	4 yards	4 yards
Binding	⅓ yard	⅓ yard	½ yard	½ yard
Low-loft cotton batting	crib	crib	twin	twin

CUT

MATERIAL	BABY *(two color)*	BABY *(multicolor)*	LAP *(two color)*	LAP *(multicolor)*
Fabric A and B	(8) 5″ x WOF* strips//subcut (60) total 5″ x 5″	—	(10) 7″ x WOF strips//subcut (60) total 7″ x 7″	—
Background Fabric	—	(8) 5″ x WOF strips//subcut (60) total 5″ x 5″	—	(10) 7″ x WOF strips//subcut (60) total 7″ x 7″
Accent Fabrics	—	(1) 5″ x WOF strip each// subcut (8) 5″ x 5″	—	(1) 7″ x WOF strip each// subcut (6) 7″ x 7″
Binding	(5) 2¼″ x WOF strips	(5) 2¼″ x WOF strips	(7) 2¼″ x WOF strips	(7) 2¼″ x WOF strips

* width of fabric

Note: Experienced quilters would likely cut 4⅞″ and 6⅞″ squares to make half-square triangle units rather than 5″ and 7″. For beginners, I recommend cutting in the dimensions outlined above, then trimming down the half-square triangle blocks after sewing.

PREPARE THE BACKING
For baby quilt, cut backing into (2) 48″ x 29″ pieces. Sew together along 48″ side using ½″ seam allowance. Set seam and press open.

For lap quilt, cut backing into (2) 68″ x 41″ pieces. Sew together along 68″ side using ½″ seam allowance. Set seam and press open.

Set finished backing aside for now.

SEW
Use ¼″ seam allowance unless otherwise noted.

HALF-SQUARE TRIANGLE BLOCKS
1. Pair one Fabric A and Fabric B square (or one background and one accent fabric), right sides together. Pin in two opposite corners to prevent shifting.

2. Mark diagonal line using clear ruler and pencil or chaco liner.

3. Sew ¼″ away from marked line. Repeat on remaining side of line.

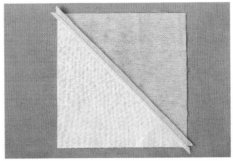

4. Press block flat to set seams. Cut on marked line to separate into two triangles; unfold triangles and voila! You have two half-triangle blocks.

5. Press seam open or to darker fabric.

Repeat Steps 1–5 with remaining squares for a total of 120 blocks.

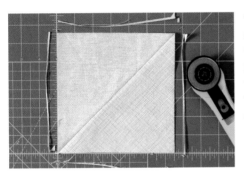

7. Trim blocks to 4½″ x 4½″ for baby quilt or 6½″ x 6½″ for lap quilt. Line up the seam on the block with the diagonal line on your clear ruler. This takes some time, but when you're sewing blocks together and they are all identical in size, you'll be glad you did!

THE PRESSING DEBATE

A hotly debated topic among quilters is which pressing method is best for seam strength, flat seams, and ease of matching points. Pressing open takes a little more time but yields a nice flat seam that some find easier to match when sewing blocks together. Pressing to the dark side is faster and some say stronger in the finished quilt, but does add bulk at seams when sewing blocks together or quilting. The important thing to me is that you press your seam, period. Trying to sew blocks together when they haven't been pressed doesn't make for a pleasant experience. Over time, you'll likely pick a personal preference in the pressing debate.

"I was intimidated at first, but quickly realized how fun it is. This project has given me a great sense of accomplishment and I'm already thinking about my next quilt!"

—CHRISTINE

THE QUILT TOP

8. Lay out blocks according to the quilt design you've chosen. Quilt will be 10 blocks wide and 12 blocks tall. Step back often, examining color placement and balance of lights and darks. Use painter's tape to label and number each row. A floor or large table works, as does an inexpensive flannel-backed vinyl tablecloth. Your blocks will stick to the flannel, allowing you to roll it up and put away your project. When you come back to it, everything will be in place.

9. Use painter's tape to number the upper left corner of the first block in every row. You will number 1–12. Snap a picture of your final layout with a digital camera or cell phone. Trust me on this

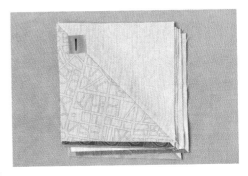

one! That picture will come in handy as you sew blocks and rows together.

10. Stack blocks for Row 1, placing first block on top and taking care to keep orientation of blocks correct as you pick up the blocks in the whole row.

11. Sew blocks together to form rows, using ¼″ seam. Your painter's tape will help you remember which block is the first in the row.

Chain Piecing: If you chose a layout from pages 150-152 marked with an asterisk as chain piece–friendly, consider chain stitching wherever possible. In this handy time-saver, you'll sew together a stack of similar blocks one right after the other, rather than stopping to trim threads after each block. Try it!

12. Set seams and press open or to one side. If pressing to one side, be sure to alternate in the next row by pressing in the opposite direction. Example: press seams in all odd numbered rows to the left and even numbered rows to the right.

13. Repeat with remaining rows, moving each finished row back to your layout to keep things organized.

14. Pin Row 1 and Row 2 right sides together. First pin at each end of the row, then at each seam, then pin in the center of those pins. Sew together, pausing often to remove pins and maintain a consistent ¼″ seam. Backstitch at both ends of the row. Set seams and press open.

15. Continue sewing rows together in pairs, then sew pairs of rows together. Continue until all rows are together as a finished quilt top.

▶ TIP

In order to make the quilt easier to handle, the final seam should be sewing two halves of the quilt together.

THE QUILT SANDWICH

16. Place backing piece right side down on flat surface. Tape opposite sides to the floor first, keeping backing taut, before taping remaining sides. Avoid carpeted areas if possible. Tile and wood floors provide excellent guidelines to keep your quilt and backing straight.

17. Layer and smooth batting over backing fabric. Be sure all wrinkles are removed.

18. Center quilt top right side up on top of batting. You may find it helpful to fold the quilt top in half, right sides together, and place it first. Then smooth and unfold the remaining half. Smooth out all wrinkles.

19. Think about and plan how your machine quilting will be done. Free motion quilting (swirls and curves) is a fantastic addition to a quilt, but can be tricky for a first timer. If this is your first quilt, straight-line quilting is recommended and outlined here. Making a quick sketch of your quilt on paper can help.

20. Pin layers together with curved safety pins. Begin at center of quilt and work to outer edges, smoothing layers along the way. Pin every 3″ to 5″ (about the size of your fist) in all directions. If possible, avoid placing pins in areas where quilting lines will go.

21. Pull up tape. Roll up quilt sandwich on opposite sides, leaving the center 12″ — to 15″ unrolled. Attach walking foot and extension table to sewing machine if desired, as we did in on page 140.

► **CHOOSING A QUILTING STYLE**

Stumped about how to quilt your quilt top? Take inspiration from the quilts from School of Sewing students. In our group, some quilted on both sides of the seam lines, some on the diagonal using painter's tape as a guide (just don't sew through it!), and some in an allover straight-line design. Use the edge of your presser foot as a guide along the seam lines. You can also use your walking foot's adjustable guide bar, as noted on page 140.

22. Begin quilting at center of one side, gradually working to an outer edge. Remove pins as you come to them and roll and unroll your quilt as needed. Ensure that the weight of the quilt is supported by an extension table or your work surface. Any extra weight in fabric hanging off the table will pull on the quilt top, making it difficult to get even stitches.

23. Trim backing and batting even with the edge of the quilt top.

24. Make and attach binding, following steps outlined in Binding 101, page 140.

25. Wash and dry your finished masterpiece for a cozy and crinkly look. Then either cuddle up on the couch or run next door to show it off to your neighbor. Yay, you! You did it! Can you believe it? I'm incredibly proud of you!

WHY A QUARTER INCH MATTERS

Quilts are made using ¼" seam allowances, and getting that magical ¼" is more important than you might think. A smaller seam allowance would not be as durable and can lead to broken seams and holes in your quilt over time. In addition, accuracy matters because a seam allowance mistake made over and over will multiply over several pieces. Entire rows will not match up, leading to puckers, mismatched seams, and a host of other problems. I suggest investing in a quarter-inch presser foot, which is a relatively low cost for the great benefits it provides.

Test your machine's accuracy by sewing (2) 2" squares of fabric together along one side. Press seams open or to one side and measure the unit. If it's not 3.5" wide, you'll need to adjust your needle to the left or right until you achieve an accurate ¼" seam. Snap a photo or make a note on painter's tape and stick it to your machine to remember these settings each time you sew.

EXTRA CREDIT

Super Speedy Half-Square Triangles: If finishing one quilt has you itching to start another, consider this fantastic time-saver. Best for two-color designs, it allows you to sew eight half-square triangle units at once!

 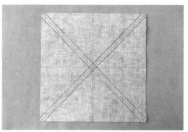 

Quilt Size: Baby, Lap

Square size to cut: 10″ x 10″, 14″ x 14″

Number of squares needed: 8 each of two fabrics, 8 each of two fabrics

1. Place two different colored squares right sides together. Mark both diagonals. Pin squares together in three or four unmarked areas.

2. Sew along both sides of each line, using ¼″ seam allowance.

3. Press to set seams.

4. Mark a vertical and horizontal line at the center of each side. Cut along all marked lines: horizontal, vertical, and both diagonal lines.

5. Open blocks and press seams open or to the darker fabric. Utterly amazing, right?

Quilt Layout Options

MULTI COLORED QUILT DESIGNS

▶ Featuring one background fabric and 8 (baby sized)
or 10 (lap sized) accent fabrics

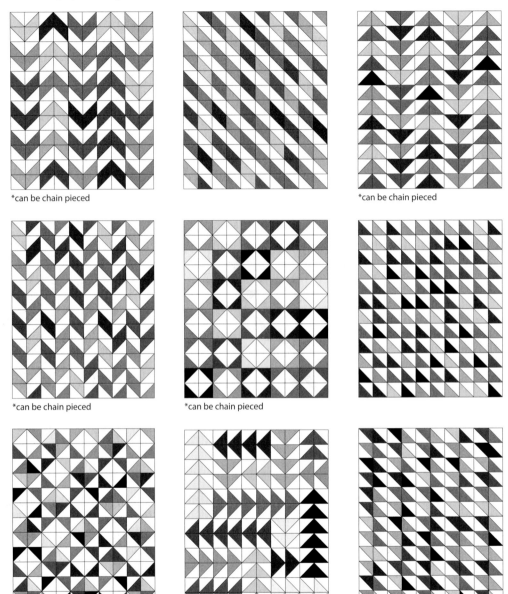

*can be chain pieced

*can be chain pieced

*can be chain pieced

*can be chain pieced

*can be chain pieced

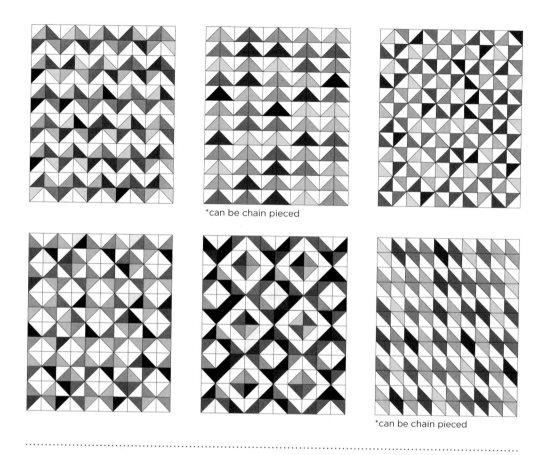

*can be chain pieced

*can be chain pieced

NO BACKGROUND FABRIC USED
Baby size: 8 lights & 8 darks. **Lap size**: 10 lights & 10 darks

TWO COLOR QUILT DESIGNS
▸ Uses only two fabrics

*all can be chain pieced

PLEASE DO NOT CUT PATTERN PIECES.

Templates

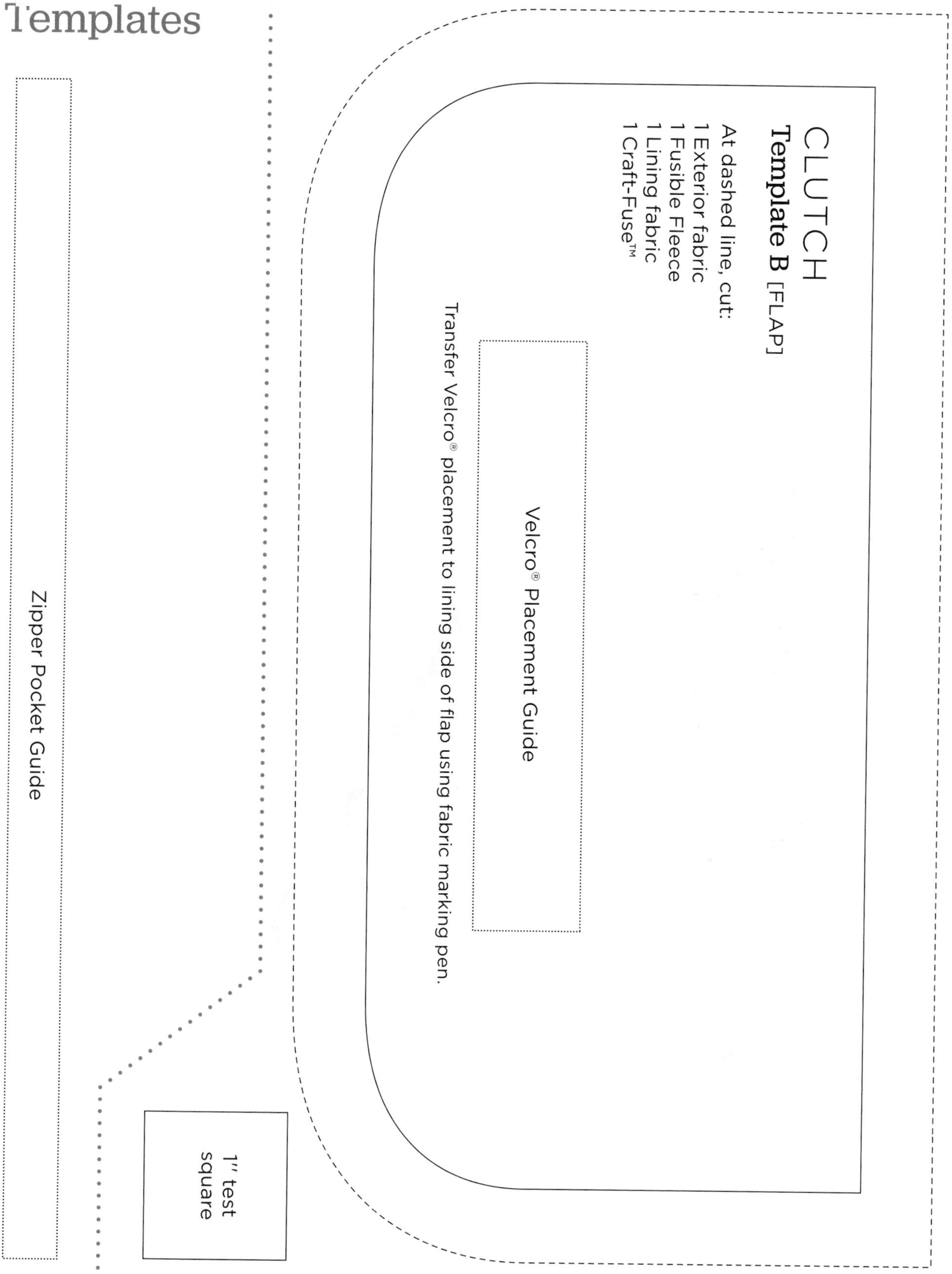

CLUTCH
Template B [FLAP]

At dashed line, cut:
1 Exterior fabric
1 Fusible Fleece
1 Lining fabric
1 Craft-Fuse™

Transfer Velcro® placement to lining side of flap using fabric marking pen.

Velcro® Placement Guide

Zipper Pocket Guide

1" test
square

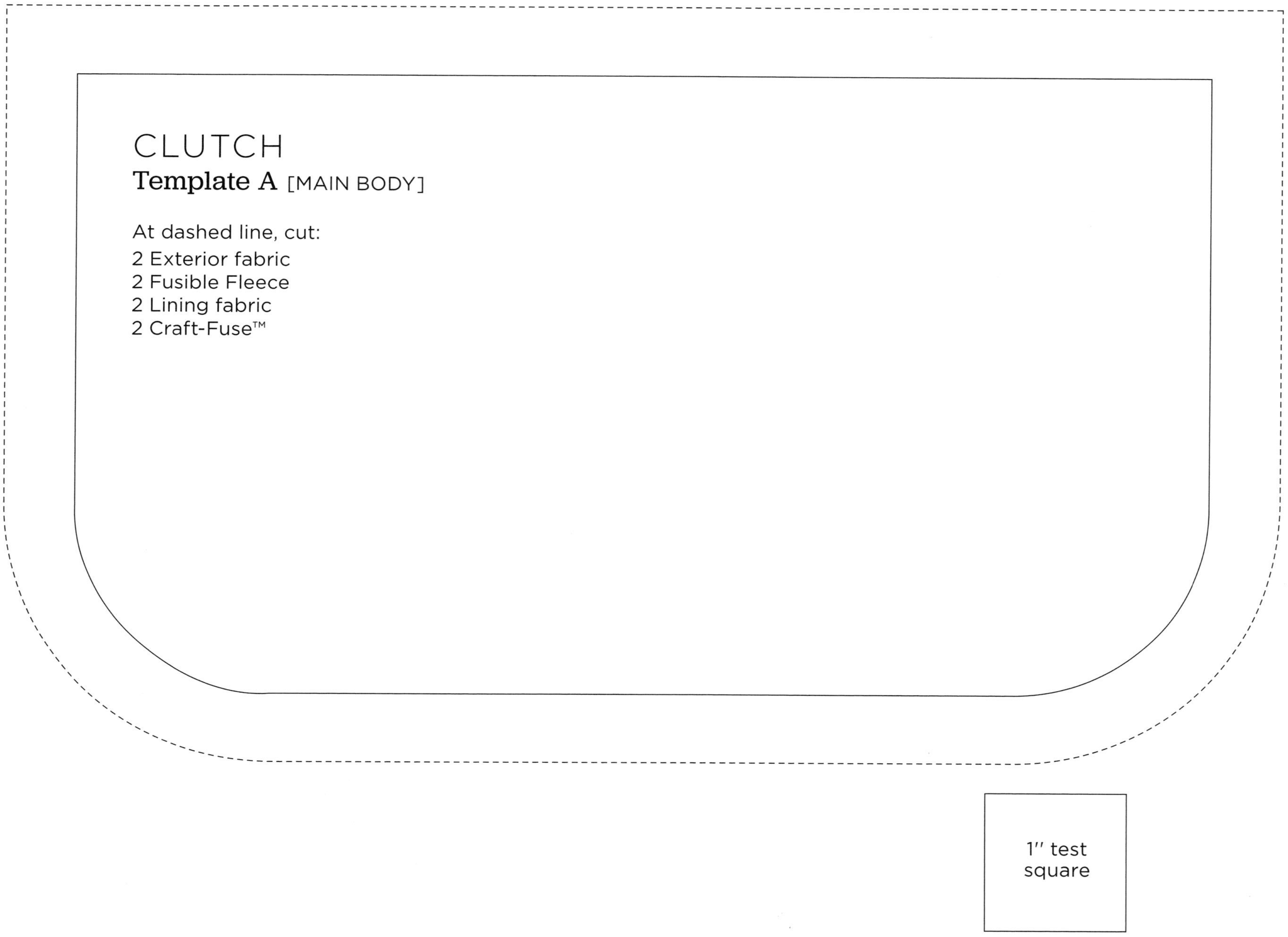

CLUTCH
Template A [MAIN BODY]

At dashed line, cut:
2 Exterior fabric
2 Fusible Fleece
2 Lining fabric
2 Craft-Fuse™

1" test square

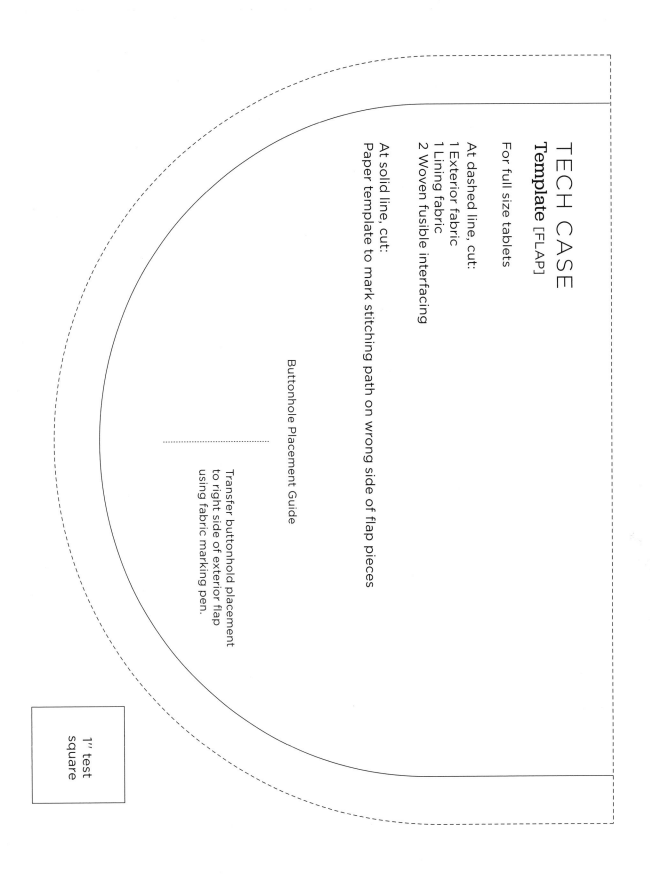

TECH CASE
Template [FLAP]

For full size tablets

At dashed line, cut:
1 Exterior fabric
1 Lining fabric
2 Woven fusible interfacing

At solid line, cut:
Paper template to mark stitching path on wrong side of flap pieces

Buttonhole Placement Guide

Transfer buttonhold placement to right side of exterior flap using fabric marking pen.

1" test
square

Glossary

Bias Tape

Because it is cut on the bias, this product can be used in straight or curved edges of projects. You can buy prepackaged or make your own using a metal bias tape maker as shown in the Simple Strings Apron.

Bias Tape Maker

One end of a strip is fed into the widest end of the bias maker and pulled through, where it exits the bias maker folded with outside edges meeting in the middle. A quick press with the iron and a lot of time is saved! These can be used with strips cut on the bias or straight of grain, which is the method shown in this book. A variety of widths are available, so be sure to find the one for the correct width of your project.

Chaco Liner

Run the wheel along the wrong side of fabric and the Chaco liner leaves a small trail of colored chalk, marking the stitching or cutting lines. A variety of colors and refill options are available.

Charm Square

A 5" square of fabric. Often sold in "charm packs," these are a nice way to get a little bit of an entire line of fabric. But it is just that: a little bit. A pack or two of these makes for an easy and speedy patchwork quilt, though, and can be used in combination with the half-square triangle block covered in the My First Quilt project.

Drape

How a fabric hangs. Especially important in garment sewing. If you've ever watched *Project Runway*, you know how much of a difference drape can make in a dress or shirt.

Elastic

Elastic comes in several widths and can be used in a wide variety of projects. Non-roll elastic is a must in waistbands.

Extension Table

A wonderful addition that you may be able to find for your machine. This elevated table fits around the bed of your machine to extend the work surface. Especially helpful when working with larger pieces of fabric or quilts. Once you use one, you'll be hooked.

Fat Eighth

A less commonly found pre-cut, fat eighths are 9" x 22" cuts of fabric.

Fat Quarter

A common pre-cut, measuring 18" x 22".

Fusible Hem Tape

Great for temporarily holding fabric in place before sewing, like in zipper placements or for holding a curtain hem in place.

Hand

Simply put, it's how the fabric feels in your hand. Is it course or soft? Thick or thin? Can you feel the threads or is it smooth?

Heat-Resistant Batting

Heat-resistant batting is used in hot pads and oven mitts. I often add a layer of regular batting to these projects, too.

Hem Guide

These are fantastic! To use them, fold the edge of your fabric to the specific hem width desired and press with the guide in place. If you plan to do much garment sewing, this tool is indispensable. In a pinch, use the Hem Paper Pressing Guides tip on page 87.

Hera Marker

Leaves a temporary crease on fabric when applied with pressure to a project. Excellent for marking quilting lines for the Set the Table Place Mats!

Hook and Eye

Most often used in garment making and placed at the upper end of a zipper pull, hook and eye pieces are also hand sewn to the project.

Interlining

Interlining is a layer between the exterior and interior of a project. You don't see this layer, but it adds thickness and strength or adds warmth. Use canvas, felt, or fleece for these purposes.

Jelly Roll Strip (Moda brand)

These 2½" x 44" strips of fabric are sold by a variety of manufacturers come in coordinating bundles of twenty to forty strips. Strip sets are popular among quilters and as a result many quilt patterns are written specifically for this pre-cut. A word of warning, though. Never pre-wash a strip set in your washing machine...unless, of course, you like untangling massive knots.

Layer Cake (Moda brand)

A 10" square, sold under the name "layer cake" or "10 square," these sets of fabrics are like a giant charm square. In fact, you can cut these in half along the length and width and create your own 5" charm squares.

Mitered Corner

When two seams or sides of binding meet at a corner in a 45-degree angle.

Measuring Tape

A staple in any sewist's toolbox, a flexible measuring tape is used for everything from clothing to quilts.

Needle Threader

If threading a hand-sewing or machine needle is tricky for you, a needle threader can make the process easier.

Paper Scissors

Use these for cutting patterns, paper-backed fusible interfacing, and other non-fabric materials.

Pinking Shears

These odd-looking scissors with zigzag-shaped blades are used to cut along the raw edge of fabric to prevent fraying. If you plan to do much garment sewing or if quilting with flannels and other fabrics that fray, you might find these handy.

Piping

Often used in pillows, piping is sewn into the seams to add a bit of finished detail. You can make your own using bias cut fabric strips and cording.

Pressing Cloth

Many types of interfacing call for the use of a pressing cloth, which is used between the project and the iron. A damp pressing cloth can improve the bond between interfacing and fabric. You can buy a pressing cloth at the fabric store, but a piece of muslin makes a perfectly good one, as well.

Ribbon

Used to add detail or embellishment to projects, ribbon comes in a wide variety of widths. Ribbon is attached to a project by sewing down the edges.

Rickrack

This can be sewn in a seam or along the outside of a project. To attach to a project, sew down the center of the rickrack.

Sleeve Board

This is essentially a miniature ironing board. Much like the seam roll, a sleeve board makes pressing narrow tubes of fabric much easier.

Snaps

Snaps can be used for everything from clothing to bags and are hand sewn in place on the project.

Tailor's Chalk

Typically used in alterations and garment sewing, tailor's chalk is a hard piece of chalk that marks seams and darts on fabric.

Thimble

To protect your fingers when hand sewing, you may want to use a thimble. Some are leather, others metal or silicone. Much to my mother's dismay, I actually don't use one.

Tracing Wheel

Best for sewists who make garments, these allow you to transfer darts and other markings from the pattern piece to your fabric.

Resources

SEWING BOOKS

Big City Bags by Sara Lawson (Martingale, 2013)

Gertie's New Book for Better Sewing by Gretchen Hirsch (STC, 2012)

Little Things to Sew by Liesl Gibson (STC, 2011)

Sew Everything Workshop by Diana Rupp (Workman, 2007)

Stitch by Stitch by Deborah Moebes (Krause, 2010)

The Collette Sewing Handbook by Sarai Mitnick (Krause, 2011)

QUILTING BOOKS

Denyse Schmidt Quilts by Denyse Schmidt (Chronicle, 2005)

Essential Guide to Modern Quilting (Lucky Spool, 2014)

Free Motion Quilting with Angela Walters by Angela Walters (Stash Books, 2012)

Modern Patchwork by Elizabeth Hartman (Stash Books, 2012)

Modern Quilts, Traditional Inspiration by Denyse Schmidt (STC, 2012)

Practical Guide to Patchwork by Elizabeth Hartman (Stash Books, 2010)

Quilting Modern by Jacquie Gering and Katie Pedersen (Interweave, 2012)

INDEPENDENT PATTERN COMPANIES

The sewing world is full of independent pattern makers. Here are a few personal favorites:

Atkinson Designs
Quilts and home decor patterns

Collette
Garment patterns with vintage style

Empty Bobbin Sewing Studio
Quilts, holiday patterns, and home accessories (shameless self-promotion!)

Oliver & S/Straight Stitch Society/ Liesl & Co
Contemporary children's clothing, accessories, and women's garment patterns

Pink Chalk Studio
Check out The Mail Sack!

Sew Sweetness
Bag patterns

FAVORITE MAGAZINES

American Patchwork & Quilting/ Quilts & More

Love Patchwork & Quilting

Modern Patchwork

Modern Quilts Unlimited

Quilty

Stitch

FAVORITE BLOGS

Pink Chalk Studio (pinkchalkstudio.com)

Sew, Mama, Sew! (sewmamasew.com)

Oh, Fransson! (ohfransson.com)

Tallgrass Prairie Studio (tallgrassprairiestudio.blogspot.com)

Handmade by Alissa (handmadebyalissa.com)

Teaginny Designs (teaginnydesigns.blogspot.com)

The Modern Quilt Guild (TheModernQuiltGuild.com)

Red Pepper Quilts (redpepperquilts.com)

Film in the Fridge (filminthefridge.com)

My Aunt June (myauntjune.blogspot.com)

Whipstitch (whip-stitch.com/blog)

Sew Sweetness (sewsweetness.com)

In Color Order (incolororder.com)

Gertie's New Blog for Better Sewing (blogforbettersewing.com)

Colletterie (colletterie.com)

MADE (danamadeit.com)

Made by Rae (made-by-rae.com)

The Long Thread (thelongthread.com)

The Purl Bee (purlbee.com)

Sewaholic (sewaholic.net)

Quilting Is My Therapy (quiltingismytherapy.com)

SEWING MACHINE REVIEWS

Pattern Review (sewing. patternreview.com/SewingMachine)

RECOMMENDED TUTORIAL & ONLINE LEARNING SITES

Better Homes & Gardens: How to Sew (howtosew.com)

Craftsy (craftsy.com)

Creative Bug (creativebug.com)

Missouri Star Quilt Company (quiltingtutorials.com)

Quilty (heyquilty.com)

Sew 4 Home (sew4home.com)

Sew, Mama, Sew! (sewmamasew. com/category/tutorials)

My Favorite Tutorials
Find suggested tutorials at theschoolofsewing.com

FABRICS USED:

See detailed lists of fabrics used throughout this book at theschoolofsewing.com

FAVORITE ONLINE FABRIC & SUPPLY SHOPS

Drygoods Design (drygoodsdesignonline.com)

Fat Quarter Shop (fatquartershop.com)

Hawthorne Threads (hawthornethreads.com)

Mood (moodfabrics.com)

Missouri Star Quilt Co. (missouriquiltco.com)

Pink Chalk Fabrics (pinkchalkfabrics.com)

Sarah's Fabrics (sarahsfabrics.com)

Sew Modern (sewmodernonline. com)

Spoonflower for custom digital printed fabric (spoonflower.com)

ZipIt a variety of zippers, including hard to find long pull zippers (etsy.com/shop/zipit)

Index